FRONTIER JUSTICE

www.contextbooks.com

Jacket design: Beau Friedlander
Interior design: Beau Friedlander and Trevor Bundy

Context Books
368 Broadway
Suite 314
New York, NY 10013

Library of Congress Cataloging-in-Publication Data

Ritter, Scott.
Frontier justice : weapons of mass destruction and the bushwhacking of
America / Scott Ritter.
p. cm.
ISBN 1-893956-47-4 (pbk. : alk. paper)
1. United States—Foreign relations—2001- 2. United States—Politics
and government—2001- 3. Bush, George W. (George Walker), 1946-
4. United States—Foreign relations—Iraq. 5. Iraq—Foreign
relations—United States. 6. Imperialism. 7. Iraq War, 2003.
8. Weapons of mass destruction—Iraq. 9. Ritter, Scott.
10. Weapons—Inspection—Iraq. I. Title.
E902.R58 2003
327.73'009'0511—dc21
2003014449

ISBN 1-893956-47-4

9 8 7 6 5 4 3 2 1

Manufactured in the United States of America

SCOTT RITTER
FORMER U.N. WEAPONS INSPECTOR

FRONTIER JUSTICE

WEAPONS OF MASS DESTRUCTION AND THE BUSHWHACKING OF AMERICA

CONTEXT BOOKS
NEW YORK
2003

Table of Contents

"Men, for years now, have been talking about war and peace. But now, no longer can they just talk about it. It is no longer a choice between violence and nonviolence in this world; it's nonviolence or nonexistence."

—Dr. Martin Luther King, Jr.

Foreword

During the months since the end of Operation Iraqi Freedom, and as the reality that there are no weapons of mass destruction in Iraq sinks in among a growing number of Americans, I have received a large number of phone calls, letters, and email messages from people around the United States and the world asking me if I felt vindicated now that the position I had taken before the war—that there was no proof these weapons existed, and as such no justification for war with Iraq—had proven to be correct. "How do you feel?" they ask. "Are you happy?"

The truth of the matter is that I am sad. There is no vindication to be had as one mourns the death of American, British, and Iraqi men and women, those who have already died, and those who will die. For the sake of my country, I hoped that I was wrong about the weapons of mass destruction, that they would be found in overwhelming numbers, so that the families and friends of those who perished or were maimed in this war might have at least the knowledge that their loss was suffered in the service of a good and just cause. I hoped that they would be found so that the honor of the nation which I dearly love would not be tarnished in such an ignoble fashion.

But the weapons were not found. The sacrifice made by so many was made in support of a cause so unjust. My nation debased itself in the pursuit of a toothless dictator who posed a threat to no one other than the people he ruled. And while the world may be better off without Saddam Hussein, it is debatable as to whether or not that truism holds for the people of Iraq, who suffer under the burden of an unjust occupation carried out by the practitioners of a new global empire. These are not the actions of the nation to which I swore allegiance. And as an American citizen and patriot, I have resolved to do something about it, which is why when Beau Friedlander and Context Books asked me to write this particular book, I jumped at the opportunity. This is a book about a lie and the liars who told it to the American people. It is also about citizenship and the responsibilities of all Americans to hold themselves to the highest standards of citizenship, including the concept of holding accountable those whom we elect to represent us in higher office. It is about truth, justice, and the rule of law, and the danger imposed on us all by those who lie, pervert justice, and absolve themselves from the rule of law.

It is also a book written by me, someone who is no stranger to controversy. There are those who question my credibility as a witness as regards the issues addressed here, who say I gave aid and comfort to the enemy by traveling to Baghdad in September of 2002, that my position "flip flopped" regarding Iraq since the time of my resignation from the United Nations in August 1998, and that I lack the moral credentials necessary to speak to the American public about the rule of law because of allegations concerning an arrest in June 2001. As such, this book is also about me to the degree necessary.

If after reading this book, I have failed to make my case, whether about myself or the actions of the Bush administration, so be it. But if you, the reader, find the arguments compelling, then it is time for some self-reflection of your own. What are you, whether a citizen of the United States of America or the world, willing to do to defend the concepts of a fair and just society?

In my travels throughout the United States and the world these past years I have witnessed a great deal of desire for peace and justice coming from a great many people. But desire, in and of itself, gets you nowhere.

One needs *will*.

Will transforms people.

Will motivates actions that can truly change the world.

We live in a world threatened by those practitioners of lies and tyranny who have the will to impose themselves on us all. The question is, do we champions of truth and justice have the will to engage this enemy and prevail? To answer that question, one must have the will to begin the journey of self-empowerment. Knowledge is the key to such an endeavor. I sincerely hope that this book, in its own small way, will be seen as a contribution.

Scott Ritter
Delmar, New York

FRONTIER JUSTICE

Chapter One The West Texas Lynch Mob

"Our country, right or wrong. When right, to be
kept right; when wrong, to be put right."
—Carl Schurz

Operation Iraqi Freedom, the recently concluded American invasion of Iraq, will go down in history as one of the most one-sided military victories in modern times. The professionalism, courage, and overall superb quality of the American armed forces was underscored during every phase of the campaign, regardless of the fact that they faced an enemy more impressive on paper than in person. The tragic cost of war, in terms of human life (American, British, and Iraqi alike), destruction of property, and expenditure of national resources, was somewhat mitigated by the rapidity with which the regime of Saddam Hussein was defeated. Many, including myself, anticipated a much longer and bloodier campaign. Thankfully this did not occur. And when, less than three weeks after the war started, U.S. Marines collaborated with a crowd of fewer than two hundred happy citizens of Baghdad to pull down the massive bronze statue of the Iraqi dictator in Firdos Square, installed with much fanfare (and at great cost) only a year earlier, it was hard, if not impossible, not to enjoy the pride and accomplishment that shone on the faces of those young Marines as they punctuated their victory. That day, the face of American patriotism truly glowed on the sweat-glistened features of those American warriors.

Military service is often cited as the quintessential act of patriotism, especially during a time of conflict. Indeed, we who wait at home while our brave soldiers, sailors, airmen, and Marines wage war in our defense are often reminded that the liberties we enjoy and cherish are paid for with the blood and sacrifice of these selfless Americans. The white markers of the graves of so many fallen dot the landscape in scores of cemeteries throughout the United States and Europe. The fact that they are often called upon to pay the highest price in this defense of the United States only underscores the depth of patriotic duty these brave men and women embrace when they put on the uniform of the American armed forces.

But we should never forget what it is our service members swear an oath to defend—with their lives, if necessary: the Constitution. Not the president of the United States, not Congress, the Pentagon, or the flag. No person, institution, or national symbol. They are sworn to defend words on a piece of parchment penned over two centuries ago. But these are no ordinary words. Rather, they represent the values and ideals which define the United States of America, as well as the terms under which we, the people of the United States, choose to live in this more perfect union we call our country. The Constitution defines the United States as a nation of law, a civilized society functioning as a democratic republic that guarantees each citizen the right to life, liberty, and the pursuit of happiness. Inherent in this social model is the concept of democratic representation, where government officials are elected by, and held accountable to, the free will of the people. It is the people of the United States who are the ultimate arbiters as to how they are governed. As President Abraham Lincoln sagely noted in his Gettysburg Address, the United States truly is "government of the people, by the people, for the people."

This concept of American citizenship, and the ultimate role the individual citizen plays in the formulation and implementation of government, represents a critical element of the foundation of our nation. One should carefully reflect on the words contained in that oath of service every member of the United States Armed Forces takes when enlisting or upon accepting a commission (it should be noted that it is the same oath all those who serve in government service take, military or civilian): "To uphold and defend the Constitution of the United States of America against all enemies, foreign and domestic."

Foreign *and* domestic. We have seen the face of patriotism on display throughout our history, whenever our nation has gone to war, on the young men and women who serve so proudly and who are all too often called upon to make the ultimate sacrifice in our defense, as they swore they would. This is the face of patriotism as it pertains to the defense of the United States against foreign enemies, and it is the one we are most familiar with. But what of the defense against domestic enemies? The Constitution specifically prohibits the United States military from participating in operations against American citizens on the soil of the United States. When the actions of American citizens or foreign nationals within the borders of the United States threaten the Constitution—and by extension, our national existence—there are a myriad of law enforcement, judicial, executive, and legislative bodies that are in place to serve and protect the national interest. Like the military, these public servants provide a framework of stability and security in which civil society functions.

But who maintains this framework? Is it sufficient for a society that stakes a claim at being democratic to simply trust in the good faith and judgement of those whom it elects to represent it in public office, or is there a need for oversight and accountability? The Constitution of the United States, while providing for the conduct of democratic society, does not set forth a blue print for the implementation of democracy. Governmental bodies legislate and execute the rules and regulations of society, and the judiciary safeguards these by making sure they are consistent with the provisions of the Constitution and the rule of law. But it is the duty and responsibility of each individual American citizen to be the watchdog of American democracy.

This system of checks and balances has served the United States well, although not perfectly, throughout its history. The judiciary for the most part only involves itself in domestic issues, leaving matters of state, including national security, in the hands of the executive and legislative branches of government. Most Americans tend to respond in kind, and as such the concept of citizen accountability and oversight on matters pertaining to war and peace rarely receives the kind of attention given to more mundane domestic matters. But is this good citizenship? If the government of the United States decides to pursue a cause in which it deems the potential sacrifice of the lives of those who serve in the military is warranted, who is responsible for monitoring the government to make sure that the cause in question is worthy of that sacrifice? The face of patriotism is often depicted as someone in uniform, far away from home, sacrificing for the freedom of the whole. But there is another face of patriotism, that of the individual American, who maintains as his or her obligation as a citizen, to continuously hold those they elect to represent them accountable for the decisions made in their name. While most Americans accept military service as the embodiment of patriotism, what they fail to realize is that those in the military are relatively powerless when it comes to protesting poorly conceived, or executed, policies concerning the utilization of force. So, who is there to protect the service member? The answer is, in short, the American citizen. Unfortunately, many Americans, in their rush to rally around the flag during times of conflict and crisis, forget the importance of citizenship, and the fact that supervision and oversight of American democracy must be constant if it is to be effective at all.

Thus the other face of patriotism—the voice of public dissent provided by the antiwar protester and the practitioner of civil disobedience, the moral compass borne by the civil liberties watchdog, the academic intellectual critic, and the various (and diverse) religious communities throughout the country, and the common citizen, quietly going about his or her daily business with one eye focused on those whom they elected to higher office and the duties they perform. These, and others—all Americans, all those dedicated to defending the same values and ideals as those who wear the uniform of the armed forces. To criticize these "other" American patriots for their service to country is to ignore the fact that the distance between totalitarian rule and democratic rule is measured by the number of citizens who actively invest themselves in participatory, versus passive, democracy. As former president Theodore Roosevelt—a man who was not noted for his temerity—once wrote, "To announce that there must be no criticism of the president, or that we are to stand by the president right or wrong, is not only unpatriotic and servile, but is morally treasonable to the American public." Lest it be forgotten, these words were penned in 1918, while the United States was fighting in World War I.

When citizens stop actively participating in democracy, they run the risk of ceding control to power elites who may not have the best interests of the republic in mind. Such power elites—corporate entities, special interest groups, political ideologues, and others—often seek to maintain their influence by convincing the citizenry that the well-being of the collective is best decided by handing power and influence to a few, and trusting in these few to do right by the majority. Power elites sometimes exploit fear and ignorance as a means of selling a given policy. In this manner, power elites seek to wrap the citizen in a cocoon of comfort and security, promising a life journey of relative peace and prosperity if the citizen agrees not to rock the boat.

But this is not citizenship—it is consumerism, and consumerism at the expense of citizenship represents the death of the American democratic republic. A good citizen does not need to take an oath of poverty to be effective. A good citizen simply needs to avoid the narcotic of unconstrained consumerism, and remember that the ultimate root of power in the United States is the individual American, empowered with knowledge that enables the politics of fear and ignorance to be overcome by rational and informed citizenship, judiciously applied. When the interests of the power elites and the republic coincide, the other face of patriotism is denigrated as obstructive and unappreciated. But when the interests of the power elites and the republic clash, it is the very obstructive nature of individual citizenship—the other face of patriotism—that preserves the integrity of the republic and that for which it stands, indivisible, with liberty and justice for all.

Operation Iraqi Freedom provides a perfect case study for the evaluation of the two faces of patriotism, and how they can, and should, complement one another: those who took an oath to defend, with their lives if necessary, the Constitution of the United States, and those who hold accountable the democratically elected officials who make the decisions to employ American military power. Unfortunately, only one face of patriotism, that of the warrior (or those who vocalize support for the warrior), has been embraced by the American public as deserving of recognition and praise. The other face of patriotism, the citizen activist, has been denigrated and mocked in many quarters as un-American, unpatriotic. The military phase of Operation Iraqi Freedom is over, and the victory has been unprecedented. The horror and crimes of the regime of Saddam Hussein have been underscored tenfold as the prisons and torture chambers are uncovered, and more and more eyewitnesses to the deposed Iraqi dictator's despotic rule come forward with their testimony. But in the rush of euphoria that accompanies the scenes of Saddam's statues toppling, his palaces crumbling, his portraits burning, Americans should never lose sight of why this war was fought—to disarm Iraq of weapons of mass destruction that threatened the American republic.

The administration of President George W. Bush made its case for war in a letter to the Security Council delivered by the U.S. Ambassador to the United Nations on March 20, 2003. The entire text of this letter is provided below:

Excellency:

Coalition forces have commenced military operations in Iraq. These operations are necessary in view of Iraq's continued material breaches of its disarmament obligations under relevant Security Council resolutions, including 1441 (2002). The operations are substantial and will secure compliance with those obligations. In carrying out these operations, our forces will take all reasonable precautions to avoid civilian casualties.

The actions being taken are authorized under existing Council resolutions, including resolution 678 (1990) and resolution 687 (1991). Resolution 687 imposed a series of obligations on Iraq, including, most importantly, extensive disarmament obligations, that were conditions of the cease-fire established under it. It has long been recognized and understood that a material breach of these obligations removes the basis of the cease-fire and revives the authority to use force under resolution 678. This has been the basis for coalition use of force in the past and has been accepted by the Council, as evidenced, for example, by the Secretary General's public announcement in January 1993 following Iraq's material breach of resolution 687 that coalition forces had received a mandate from the Council to use force according to resolution 678.

Iraq continues to be in material breach of its disarmament obligations under resolution 687, as the Council affirmed in resolution 1441. Acting under the authority of Chapter VII of the U.N. Charter, the Council unanimously decided that Iraq has been and remained in material breach of its obligations and recalled its repeated warnings to Iraq that it will face serious consequences as a result of its continued violations of its obligations. The resolution then provided Iraq a "final opportunity" to comply, but stated specifically that violations by Iraq of its obligations under resolution 1441 to present a currently accurate, full and complete declaration of all aspects of its weapons of mass destruction programs and to comply with and cooperate fully in the resolution's implementation would constitute a further material breach.

The government of Iraq decided not to avail itself of its final opportunity under resolution 1441 and has clearly committed additional violations. In view of Iraq's material breaches, the basis for the cease-fire has been removed, and use of force is authorized under resolution 678.

Iraq repeatedly has refused, over a protracted period of time, to respond to diplomatic overtures, economic sanctions, and other peaceful means designed to help bring about Iraqi compliance with its obligations to disarm and to permit full inspection of its WMD and related programs. The actions that coalition forces are undertaking are an appropriate response. They are necessary steps to defend the United States and the international community from the threat posed by Iraq and to restore international peace and security in the area. Further delay would simply allow Iraq to continue its unlawful and threatening conduct.

It is the Government of Iraq that bears full responsibility for the serious consequences of its defiance of the Council's decisions. I would be grateful if you could circulate the text of this letter as a document of the Security Council.

Sincerely,
John D. Negroponte

What is most instructive about this letter is that it is a legal document which sets forth the justification, under international law, for the U.S.-led invasion of Iraq. Rather than divorce the United States from the primacy of international law, the letter from Ambassador Negroponte recognizes the binding nature of international law as set forth in the United Nations Charter. Curiously, there is no mention in this letter of "liberation" or "regime change," catch phrases used repeatedly by those who are supportive of military action against Iraq, both in and out of the Bush administration. The main reason these phrases are missing is that they have no standing under international law as set forth in the Charter of the United Nations. Given that the United States is a signatory to the United Nations Charter, and that Article 6 of the United States Constitution states that "all treaties made, or which shall be made, under the authority of the United States, shall be the supreme law of the land," acting in violation of the United Nations Charter is not only a violation of international law, but by extension, a circumvention of the law of the United States according to the Constitution.

As such, the sole legal justification for the American-led invasion of Iraq rests on the status of Iraq's disarmament obligation as set forth under relevant Security Council resolutions. If Iraq has no weapons of mass destruction, how can the United States maintain that Iraq is in material breach of its obligation to disarm as so forcefully pointed out in Ambassador Negroponte's letter to the Security Council? The citing of other existing Security Council resolutions by Mr. Negroponte is likewise curious. Resolution 678 (1990) does in fact authorize the international community to use military force against Iraq, but only to liberate Kuwait, which was invaded by Iraq in August 1990. Resolution 678 (1990) provided the legal justification for Operation Desert Storm in early 1991. It does not, however, provide any legitimacy for the initiation of military action against Iraq in connection with Resolution 687 (1991), or any other resolution.

Security Council resolutions are carefully crafted documents, and every word has meaning. It is instructive, therefore, to examine the verbiage penned by those who drafted the documents cited by Ambassador Negroponte. Paragraph 33 of resolution 687 (1991) states that the Security Council

"Declares that, upon official notification by Iraq to the Secretary General and to the Security Council of its acceptance of the provisions above, a formal cease-fire is effective between Iraq and Kuwait and the Member States cooperating with Kuwait in accordance with resolution 678 (1990)." It is important to note that Iraq did notify the Secretary General and the Security Council, in May 1991, that it intended to abide by its obligations under resolution 687 (1991), so the cease-fire went into effect. Paragraph 34 of resolution 687 (1991) says that the Security Council "Decides to remain seized of the matter and to take such further steps as may be required for the implementation of the present resolution and to secure peace and security in the area." There is no automatic trigger for the resumption of military action against Iraq. The Security Council noted that it will convene and discuss any future developments before deciding on what course of action needs to be taken.

Ambassador Negroponte's interpretation of the council's resolutions, in which he states, "It has long been recognized and understood that a material breach of these obligations removes the basis of the cease-fire and revives the authority to use force under resolution 678 (1990)," is fundamentally flawed. Clearly this is not the case. The council decided to "remain seized of the matter." Subsequent action against Iraq would, as such, require additional authorization by the council. The 1993 public announcement by the Secretary General, as cited by Mr. Negroponte, carries no weight under the law. The Secretary General cannot over rule Security Council resolutions, especially those passed under Chapter VII of the Charter. Only the council can do this, and it never did. So even the citing by Ambassador Negroponte of the council's statement in resolution 1441 (2002) of Iraq being in material breach did not constitute an automatic trigger for military action.

Mr. Negroponte's conclusion that the actions undertaken by the United States "are necessary steps to defend the United States and the international community from the threat posed by Iraq and to restore international peace and security in the area," ring hollow, especially given the fact that no weapons of mass destruction have been discovered by the U.S.-led coalition inside occupied Iraq. During the months leading up to the war with Iraq, the American people (and the world) were repeatedly told by an aggressively positive Bush administration that the Iraqi regime led by Saddam Hussein possessed massive quantities of prohibited chemical, biological, and nuclear weapons, as well as dozens of long-range ballistic missiles that were ready to deliver this deadly arsenal to Iraq's neighbors, threatening international peace and security. Furthermore, we were told that these weapons, if they fell into the hands of anti-American terror organizations, directly threatened the security of the American homeland. Saddam Hussein's regime, we were informed, was a state sponsor of terror, and had ties to terror groups who wished the United States harm. It was impossible for the president of the United States, the White House told us, to stand by idly while this threat manifested itself inside Iraq. Not only has the American occupying power inside Iraq failed to find any weapons of mass destruction, but the terror link so loudly proclaimed to exist has likewise vanished into thin air.

And yet Baghdad has fallen, and Iraq today is governed under the heel of an occupying American military boot. Like an aggressive prosecutor, the Bush administration pressed charges against the regime of Saddam Hussein for the crime of violating the United Nation's directives that Iraq disarm, and demanded that the international community convict and, moreover, seek the foreign relations equivalent of the death penalty—military action designed to remove Saddam Hussein from power. But the prosecution ran into a problem—the court authorized to hear this case, the United Nations Security Council, disagreed with the specifics of the charges, and would not move forward until due process was served. The Security Council had assigned its own investigatory body, U.N. weapons inspectors, to pursue the issue of Iraq's disarmament, and the results, while mixed, sustained neither the charges brought forward by the United States, nor the desired penalties. Rather than accept the rule of law, the Bush administration decided to take matters into its own hands. Declaring the United Nations unable or unwilling to enforce its own law, the Bush administration carried out its version of a west Texas lynch mob, breaking into the jail, pushing aside the sheriff, and stringing up the suspect by the neck until dead. Like a rancher bringing vigilante justice to a cattle rustler, the Bush administration decided that the suspect was guilty and saw no need to wait for the courts to decide.

The problem is that the hanging is over, and Rancher Bush and his west Texas lynch mob can't find the cattle supposedly rustled. It turns out Black Bart (*i.e.*, Saddam) wasn't a cattle thief at all, and that there was no justification for stringing him up. And while no one is trying to make the case that Black Bart was a good man, the community is left averting its eyes from the still warm body swinging from the nearest tree, trying to come to grips with the fact that the only crime committed here was the murder carried out by Rancher Bush and his posse.

There is a reason why the United States brought an end to vigilante rule over a hundred years ago—it is anathema to civilized society. Frontier justice was replaced with a system of laws governing the interaction between citizens and communities, as envisioned by our founding fathers when they framed the Constitution over two hundred and twenty years ago. This system of law has, through the form of binding international treaties and agreements, extended itself into how the United States, as a civilized nation, interacts with the global community of nations. The United Nations Charter, imperfect as it may be, codifies these laws. Key among the concepts contained within the Charter is the notion that the community of nations rejects war as a means of resolving their disputes. The Charter does recognize conditions in which nations may find themselves at war. Legitimate self-defense is one (as set forth in Article 51 of the Charter), and collective security (as determined by the Security Council in accordance with Chapter VII of the Charter) is another.

Rancher Bush played footloose and fancy free with the law in authorizing the lynching of Saddam Hussein. He spoke of the need for pre-emptive self-defense against a developing threat known to be hostile to the United States—Saddam's weapons of mass destruction in the hands of anti-American international terrorists. He cited the concept of collective security to confront the danger posed by Iraq's weapons of mass destruction, and the need for the United States to act when the international community failed to recognize and respond appropriately to such a threat. Of course, had the American occupying powers in Iraq found weapons of mass destruction, or a viable link between Saddam Hussein's regime and Osama bin Laden's al Qaeda terror network, then the American case would have been much stronger, and the world may have embraced frontier justice, west Texas style, as a necessary action in the face of an unresponsive court. But Rancher Bush was wrong. No weapons, no terror link—no threat. The American occupiers of Iraq have now brought into their custody the key figures involved in the Iraqi weapons of mass destruction programs, and they are all singing the same tune—there were no weapons, no program to produce such weapons. Senior Iraqi intelligence officials fingered by Rancher Bush and his posse of vigilantes as having headed a program of cooperation with Osama bin Laden are saying the same thing—there was no such link. The Bush administration says that the Iraqis are lying. However, I cannot fathom why the Iraqis would sustain such falsehoods when it would be in their best interest, in terms of receiving preferential treatment at the hands of their American captors, to come clean.

The truth of the matter is that the Bush administration has lied about Iraqi weapons of mass destruction and the Iraqi links to Osama bin Laden's al Qaeda. The Bush administration worked the lynch mob up into a murderous frenzy by fabricating evidence and misrepresenting facts. In lying to the American people, the United States Congress, and the international community, the Bush administration has demonstrated flagrant disregard for the rule of law and the very virtues of American society. As a result of this perfidy, we

Americans face a critical moment in our nation's history. How we as a people respond will dictate how we are governed, and how we interact with the rest of the world, for years to come. Do we challenge the Bush administration's brazen violation of the law, holding those elected to higher office accountable for what they have done in our name, and as such preserving the concepts, values, and ideals inherent in a democratic republic? Or do we endorse the vigilante actions of Rancher Bush's west Texas lynch mob, turning a blind eye to the criminal actions of a man, and an administration, that have protected themselves with a bodyguard of lies?

The choice is simple, and the moment of decision draws near. While it may not prove possible to evict President Bush from office through enacting articles of impeachment for high crimes and misdemeanors (how else does one describe the deaths of over two hundred Americans and many thousands of Iraqis through an illegal war of aggression?), the American people do have the power to vote for regime change in 2004. The battle for Baghdad may be over, but the battle for America has just begun.

To quote an American patriot from two centuries past, "If they want a fight, Boys, let it begin here."

Let it begin.

Chapter Two A September Night in Baghdad

> "In the beginning of a change, the Patriot is a scarce man, brave, hated, and scorned. When his cause succeeds however, the timid join him, for then it costs nothing to be a Patriot."
>
> —Mark Twain

Baghdad Conference Center, Baghdad, Iraq
September 8, 2002

The Iraqi Government Mercedes sedan came to a halt in front of the Baghdad Conference Center, completing the short drive from the Al Rasheed Hotel just across the street. An Iraqi official opened the door, and I stepped out. Just the week before I had been back in my home in upstate New York competing in a Labor Day golf tournament. Now I found myself halfway around the world, in the capital city of

Saddam Hussein's Iraq, preparing to address the Iraqi National Assembly. Ostensibly the representative body of the Iraqi people, the Iraqi National Assembly was in fact nothing more than a rubber-stamp vehicle for sustaining the rule of Iraq's only political party, the Ba'athists, under the iron grip of the Iraqi dictator.

An Iraqi official from the National Assembly ushered me through the entrance, and into the anteroom, where I met the Deputy Speaker of the Assembly. "Welcome, Mr. Scott," the official said, all smiles. "We are ready for your presentation." We proceeded down the hall before turning left into the main conference room. My entry was greeted with the strobe-like effect of multiple flash bulbs popping off, as well as the constant, blinding glare of the lights from a dozen or more news cameras. The media had announced its presence with a flourish. I did my best to suppress a smile. The room was full of journalists. My plan was working.

I strode towards the raised dais at the far end of the conference room where a table had been placed to serve as the stage from which my act of global theater was about to unfold. I had no pretensions about the nature of the body I was about to address. Saddam Hussein's Iraq was not a democratic society, and this body had no deliberative powers regarding the formulation or implementation of policy. The speech I was about to make, although delivered to the Iraqi National Assembly, was intended for a wider audience—the American people, their elected representatives, and the inner circle of Saddam Hussein's government. After a brief introduction by the leader of the Assembly, I took center stage.

"Thank you, Mr. President," I started, nodding towards the senior Iraqi present, "and the members of the Iraqi

National Assembly for giving me the opportunity to speak with you today. I understand that I appear before you today not only as the first American citizen to address your body, but also as the first nongovernmental speaker as well. And I thank you for providing me with this historical opportunity."

"This historical opportunity" was the product of a plan I had put in motion in the latter half of August 2002, after watching with increasing frustration the hearings on Iraq carried out by the Senate Foreign Relations Committee, chaired by Senator Joe Biden (D–Delaware), which had taken on all the characteristics of a Stalinist kangaroo court. Armed with a pre-ordained finding that Iraq presented a threat to the security of the United States through its continued defiance of United Nations resolutions, Senator Biden had summoned a carefully selected series of witnesses who provided alarming, if unsubstantiated, testimony to that effect. I had been lobbying hard throughout the summer for the convening of a hearing that would engage the Senate's designated oversight body in a public debate about Iraq and elicit the informed consent of the American people on a policy regarding Saddam Hussein's regime. But the hearing Senator Biden was presiding over bore no resemblance to such an event, and I was growing increasingly concerned that the American people were being subjected to a deliberate program of deception regarding the true state of Iraq's weapons of mass destruction and the threat they posed to the United States.

"As you are well aware," I continued, "we live in dangerous times, with the threat of war looming on the horizon and the harsh reality of life without normalcy stalking your nation, and indeed the entire Middle East, on a daily basis for well over a decade." I was looking at the assembled members of the Iraqi parliament seated before me, fully aware that I was in their country and needed to acknowledge their presence. But the very fact that I was in Iraq needed to be explained to another audience as well—my fellow Americans back in the United States, who might not understand what I was trying to do through this bit of global theater. "I am here today to discuss this situation with you and share with you my own personal insights and observations as to how this situation might be improved. Before I continue, I would like to offer a word or two about why I am here today and what motivates me to speak before you and the people of Iraq in this manner."

I could never allow myself to forget who my primary target audience was—my fellow Americans. Even if I were able to pull off what I was hoping to accomplish here in Iraq, all would be for naught if I couldn't sell this to a domestic American audience. "For more than twelve years now," I continued, "I have been involved with issues pertaining to Iraq. First as an officer of the United States Marine Corps participating in combat operations during the Gulf War of 1990–1991, and then as a U.N. weapons inspector—a position in which I served for nearly seven years, from 1991 to 1998—and for the past five years as an advocate of truth in the search for a peaceful resolution to the problems that plague the relations between my country and yours. I appear to you as a private citizen of the United States of America. And while I have a great deal of respect and sympathy for the people of Iraq, I have a greater love for my own country and my people, which is why I am here." I went on:

> My country seems on the verge of making a historical mistake, one that will forever change the political dynamic which

has governed the world since the end of the Second World War; namely, the foundation of international law as set forth in the United Nations Charter, which calls for the peaceful resolution of problems between nations. My government has set forth on a policy of unilateral intervention that runs contrary to the letter and intent of the United Nations Charter.

The consequences of such action are not only dire in terms of their near-term consequences as measured by death, destruction, and lost opportunities, but also the long-term global destabilization that will result from the rejection of an international law by the world's most powerful nation. As someone who counts himself as a fervent patriot and a good citizen of the United States of America, I feel I cannot stand by idly while my country behaves in such a fashion. Americans are a good people. No. Americans are a great people capable of doing great good. Never forget this. There has been a disturbing tendency among certain nations, Iraq included, to try and make a distinction between the people of the United States and the government of the United States. This is wrong. Ultimately, there is no difference, and indeed there can be no difference between the people of the United States and the government of the United States, because thanks to our constitution, we the people of the United States of America are the government. In America today, we take very seriously the concept of government of the people, by the people and for the people. This represents the very foundation of the democratic way of life we love and cherish. And you do us a great disservice if you think and say otherwise. Because ours is a government of the people, we are not only capable of all the good that humans are capable of doing, but also to be afflicted by the flaws of human nature. While I love

and cherish my country and our way of life, I am fully con-
scious of the reality that we are capable of making mistakes. I
truly believe that in the case of our current policy in Iraq, we
are fundamentally wrong.

I had drafted these words only the night before, bouncing
along a desolate stretch of highway between Amman, Jordan,
and Baghdad, Iraq. The day prior to that I had been in South
Africa, where I met the deputy prime minister of Iraq, Tariq
Aziz, and Presidential Advisor for Foreign Affairs Ghanim al-
Douri, to discuss the possibility of my addressing the Iraqi
National Assembly. Tariq Aziz was in Johannesburg to attend
the World Summit, as well as to undergo surgery to place a
stint in his coronary artery. He did not look well but was still
full of the insightfulness that made him such a formidable
opponent. Now that I was actively trying to enlist him to my
cause, his probing nature didn't let up a bit. "Why the
National Assembly, Mr. Scott?" he asked. "They have no
power. Wait until I return to Iraq, after September 15, and I
will be able to see you along with other decision makers in
Iraq."

My problem was that September 15 was too late. The
president of the United States was preparing to meet in
Crawford, Texas, with British Prime Minister Tony Blair, on
Sunday, September 8, in what was being described in certain
circles as a "war conference." This meeting was a prelude to
the President's pilgrimage on September 11 to the Pentagon,
a remote field in southern Pennsylvania, and the World Trade
Center site in New York City, where he would mark the one-
year anniversary of the horrible attack on the United States by

the forces of international terror. My concern was that the president wasn't so much trying to honor the dead as he was trying to build up war fever and fan it into a murderous rage he could use to support his plans for war with Iraq. I was deeply concerned about the speech the president was scheduled to deliver on September 12 to the General Assembly of the United Nations, where he would, in a similar fashion, exploit the tragedy of the terror attacks to bully the world body into legitimizing his personal vendetta against Saddam Hussein.

"Mr. Deputy Prime Minister," I said, "we don't have the luxury of waiting until September 15. The president of the United States is preparing to unleash the forces of blind patriotic fervor in support of a war against Iraq. I'm not here so much because I am concerned about the people of Iraq, but rather because I am concerned about what such a war would mean to the people of the United States. It is in both of our interests to prevent such a war. I'm afraid that if the president can move seamlessly from his war conference with Tony Blair, to exploit the fear and ignorance of the American people on the occasion of the first anniversary of the September 11 attacks, to a bullying performance before the United Nations on September 12, he will set in motion events that cannot be stopped, and which will lead to a war that will not only destroy your country physically, but my country morally. I need to launch a pre-emptive strike, and to accomplish that I need a global stage. A presentation before the Iraqi National Assembly would attract the attention of the international media. I need to do this before Sunday, September 8, so that when the sun rises in the United States and the president sends out his representatives to flood the Sunday morning talk shows, they have something different to talk about than simply pounding the war drums in for Iraq."

Tariq Aziz, an old-time political operator himself and someone intimately familiar with the public relations aspect of American governance, understood.

So I found myself in Baghdad, desperately trying to put voice to a message that would give pause to those about to hear the rhetoric of fear and vengeance voiced by the American commander in chief. "In the past decade there have been many mistakes made regarding the interaction between Iraq, the United States, and the United Nations. There is more than enough blame to spread around regarding this situation, including among you, the leaders of Iraq." I had put my marker on the table—we're all in this together, and we're all to blame for the fact that we're here to begin with. "But the focus on the errors of the past will not help move the current situation forward in a useful manner. Instead, we must concentrate on the present situation and how to get ourselves out of the dire situation we collectively face." I continued:

> My government is making a case for war against Iraq that is built upon the rhetoric of fear and ignorance as opposed to the reality of truth and fact. We, the people of the United States, are told repeatedly that we face a grave and imminent risk to our national security from a combination of past irresponsible behavior on the part of Iraq; ongoing efforts by Iraq to reacquire chemical, biological, and nuclear weapons, as well as long-range ballistic missiles to deliver these so-called weapons of mass destruction, which have been banned since

1991 by a Security Council resolution; and Iraq's status as a state sponsor of terror, especially alleged links between Iraq and the forces of terror that perpetrated the horrific attack against the United States on September 11 of last year.

Let me make myself perfectly clear, if Iraq acts in an aggressive manner against one of its neighbors, launching an unprovoked attack against the territory of a sovereign state, and if Iraq continues to possess weapons of mass destruction more than ten years after the international community banned these weapons, or if Iraq was any way involved in the attacks against the United States on September 11 of last year, then I would fully concur with those who said that Iraq is a rogue nation that represents a clear and present risk to international peace and security that must be dealt with harshly. Indeed, I would volunteer my services in such a struggle.

However, the rhetoric of fear that is disseminated by my government and others has not to date been backed up by hard facts that substantiate any allegations that Iraq is today in possession of weapons of mass destruction or has links to terror groups responsible for attacking the United States. Void of such facts all we have is speculation and there is no basis under international law for a nation to go to war against another nation based on speculation alone.

We are facing a crisis in America, where the politics of fear have clouded the collective judgment of the people of the United States to the point where we, unfortunately, are willing to accept at face value almost any allegation of wrongdoing on the part of Iraq without first demanding to know the factual basis of such an allegation. While this is wrong, dangerously so, let me try to put into perspective why this is the case today.

In three days, the United States will mark the one-year anniversary of an event that scarred the psychological persona of my country, the terrorist attacks of September 11 that killed nearly 3,000 innocent Americans in the span of one hundred minutes. I know Iraqis suffered much greater losses and withstood equally horrific suffering over the past decade through the combined effects of economic sanctions and war. And I am not trying to put a greater worth on the value of an American life over that of an Iraqi civilian, or any other human being for that matter. But I am trying to help explain the phenomenon that is taking place today inside the United States that allows war fever to catch on in such a rampant manner. Because of September 11, we are a nation fearful of the unknown and more easily prone to exploitation by those with agendas other than legitimate self-defense who play upon these fears.

This is the fear of the ignorant, the ill-informed, those not empowered by the facts of a given situation. I've told you that the American people are a great people who ultimately want to do good. In order for this to happen, however, we must find a way to overcome the politics of fear and those who practice it. The best way to do this is to embrace the truth. In regards to the current situation between Iraq and the United States, truth is on the side of Iraq.

Journalists were scrambling madly to write down what I was saying, and no one was leaving the conference hall. So far, so good. But now came the tough part of the presentation—debunking the president's claim that Iraq posed a threat.

The truth of the matter is that Iraq today is not a threat to its neighbors and is not acting in a manner which threatens anyone outside of its own borders. When speaking of international law as set forth by the United Nations Charter it is impossible to come up with any scenario today that would justify military action against Iraq based upon its current behavior.

The truth of the matter is that Iraq has not been shown to possess weapons of mass destruction, either in terms of having retained prohibited capability from the past or by seeking to re-acquire such capability today.

There remain concerns as to the final disposition of Iraq's past proscribed weapons programs, but these concerns are almost exclusively technical in nature and do not overcome the reality that Iraq, during nearly seven years of continuous inspection activity by the United Nations, had been certified as being disarmed to a 90 to 95 percent level, a figure which includes all of the factories used by Iraq to produce weapons of mass destruction, together with the associated production equipment, as well as the vast majority of the products produced by these factories.

The unaccounted-for material in itself does not constitute a viable weapons capability. And while the inability to achieve a final accounting is of concern and must be addressed, it is mitigated by the fact that for four years—from 1994 until 1998—the United Nations weapons inspectors monitored Iraq's permitted industrial infrastructure with the most intrusive on-site inspections regime in the history of arms control and never once found any evidence of either retained proscribed capability or efforts by Iraq to reconstitute prohibited capability that had been eliminated by the inspectors. All of this was done with the full cooperation of Iraq.

The truth of the matter is that Iraq is not a sponsor of the kind of terror perpetrated against the United States on September 11, and in fact is active in suppressing the sort of fundamentalist extremism that characterizes those who attacked the United States on that horrible day.

This is the truth, and once the American people become familiar with and accept this truth, the politics of fear will be defeated and the prospect of war between our two countries greatly diminished. Iraq needs to help the people of the United States, and indeed the world, become familiar with these truths.

Over the course of the summer I had interacted with an interesting company known as SAVE! (Surviving Any Violent Encounter), whose CEO and founder, Peter Letterese, found my analysis of Iraq—not just the product, but the methodology, as well—interesting and in keeping with the underlying philosophy of his company and what they taught. As I soon found out, SAVE! was more than simply a self-defense class, but rather a comprehensive approach to problem solving that had application across a broad spectrum of life experiences. The logo for SAVE! shows a man, arms wide, breaking free from chains that had bound him. This posture was known in the SAVE! lexicon as a "welcoming posture," and represented one of the core tenants of what Peter was trying to teach— most problems can be resolved simply by adopting a nonthreatening posture, both physically and in terms of attitude. I found this aspect of the SAVE! training to be quite relevant to what I was trying to accomplish in Iraq, and decided to incorporate it into my presentation.

"In order to do this," I continued my presentation, focusing as I was on the need for people to condition themselves to accept the truth about Iraq, "Iraq needs to adopt a more welcoming posture to invite the kind of scrutiny that would facilitate the discovery of these truths, for good reason." I pressed the point, addressing some of the underpinnings of the "welcoming posture" philosophy:

Iraq today finds itself in a defensive posture preparing itself for war. This is understandable. However, a defensive posture enables those who promote the politics of fear to distort reality in a way that turns Iraq's defensive characteristics into aggressive intent. A welcoming posture, on the other hand, would have Iraq open its arms, not in a sign of surrender but rather in a sign of embrace, one that could dispel any efforts to cast Iraq as a threat worthy of war.

Embrace the American people, especially now in their time of sorrow and pain. Let the United States know that Iraq has the greatest sympathy for the suffering felt by those who lost their loved ones on September 11, and that Iraq condemns any and all who attack innocents in such a manner. Educate the people of the United States that while Iraqis are by and large a Muslim people, they do not support the cause of those who pervert Islam, and that Iraq is in fact a bulwark against the spread of this very sort of fundamentalist extremism which characterizes those who attacked the United States.

Let America and the world know that Iraq, instead of being on the side of those who perpetrated the crimes of September

11, is in fact at one with the world community in condemning such actions and that Iraq is prepared to stand shoulder to
shoulder with the rest of the world in combating such persons
and organizations.

In addition to addressing the psychological issues associated
with gaining the trust of the American people and the international community via a "welcoming posture" policy, I knew
that even if Iraq agreed to allow for the unconditional return
of weapons inspectors, the detractors of any peaceful resolution of the Iraqi crisis would raise other issues designed to
divert public opinion away from any discussion of Iraqi compliance. These issues—the Palestinian-Israeli conflict,
Kuwait's borders, and human rights—needed to be raised in
my speech or else I would stand accused of trying to paper
over Iraq's difficult record concerning these and other issues.
"Iraq must renounce violence and aggression against all of its
neighbors," I said. Navigating the controversial issue of Israel
while speaking in the heart of Baghdad is never an easy task,
and I tackled it with as much diplomacy as I could muster.
"Iraq should let the American people and the world know
that if there is a resolution to the Palestinian crisis that is
acceptable to the people of Palestine, Iraq will accept this; that
Iraq cannot be more Palestinian than the Palestinians. And
that, in any case, Iraq rejects the threat or use of force in
resolving this crisis." I continued:

Iraq must show the people of the United States that it will act
in a manner respectful of international borders and agreements and that Iraq will strive to adhere to the international-

ly accepted standards of human rights. Educate the world as to the great good that Iraq has achieved in the past regarding health, education, and an acceptable standard of living, and convince the world that Iraq will continue to pursue these achievements in a manner which does not oppress the rights of any individuals or groups of people inside Iraq.

In the Marine Corps we were taught the concepts of maneuver warfare, of positioning yourself to maximize your strength against the enemy's weaknesses at a time and place of your choosing. I viewed my visit to Baghdad as a decisive battle in support of what I termed "waging peace." Like a military commander marshaling my forces, I was ready to deliver the decisive blow. All of my efforts would be for naught if I failed in getting Iraq to agree to the unconditional return of weapons inspectors. So far, in my presentation, I had been carrying out what a military practitioner of maneuver warfare would term "preparation of the battlefield." Now it was the time to engage on the main issue—weapons inspections.

"And," I said with as much gravity as I could master, "most importantly, show the world that Iraq does not possess weapons of mass destruction. Iraq must loudly reject any intention of possessing these weapons and then work within the framework of international law to demonstrate this as a reality." I took a breath, and waded into the heart of my argument:

> There is only one way that Iraq can achieve this, with the unconditional return of U.N. weapons inspectors, allowing such inspectors unfettered access to sites inside Iraq in order

to complete the disarmament tasks as set forth in Security Council resolutions. On this matter, Iraq has no choice. Any effort made by Iraq to block the return of inspectors and any conditions placed by Iraq on the work of the inspectors will only be used by those who seek to exploit the politics of fear by twisting these actions into the perception that Iraq somehow has something to hide and as such is a threat to international peace and security.

Let me be very clear. The only path towards peace that will be embraced by the international community is one that begins by Iraq agreeing to the immediate, unconditional return of U.N. weapons inspections, operating in full keeping with the mandate as set forth by existing U.N. Security Council Resolutions. Nothing else will be acceptable. Iraq cannot attempt to link the return of weapons inspectors with any other issues, regardless of justification. Unconditional return. Unfettered access. This is the only acceptable option.

I had traveled extensively in the six months leading up to this moment, both across the United States and around the globe, and knew that the gap of mistrust between Iraq and the international community, including the United States, was both wide and difficult to bridge. Like any problem, this one was best dealt with head-on. The issue wasn't Iraqi acceptance of weapons inspectors or Iraq's willingness to disarm; the issue was America's policy of regime removal, and our demonstrated willingness to use U.N.-mandated weapons inspections to facilitate this, even at the expense of corrupting the integrity of the inspection process itself.

"I know as well as any," I said, "that the inspection regime of the past for which I served was in the end corrupted by those who chose to use the unique access granted to weapons inspectors for purposes other than those set forth by the Security Council mandate. And that those inspections were used to deliberately provoke a crisis that, in turn, was used to justify the continuation of economic sanctions that continued to plague Iraq as well as acts of military aggression." I went on:

I know that weapons inspectors were used to collect information pertaining to the security of Iraq and its leadership that had nothing to do with the mandate of disarmament and everything to do with facilitating the unilateral policy objectives of those who sought to interfere in the internal politics of Iraq in a matter totally inconsistent with international law and the mandate of the Security Council governing the work of inspectors.

I know that weapons inspectors are not at work in Iraq today, not because the Iraqis kicked them out, but rather that they were ordered out by former executive chairman of the weapons inspection regime Richard Butler under pressure from the United States and without the permission of the Security Council, in order to clear the way for a military aggression in December 1998, which was triggered by Mr. Butler's inaccurate and misleading reporting concerning allegations of Iraqi noncooperation with weapon inspectors, when it was in fact the weapons inspectors who were noncompliant by unilaterally throwing away agreements governing the conduct of inspections.

I know that the vast majority of the more than one hundred targets bombed by the United States and Great Britain during Desert Fox had nothing to do with weapons production capability, but rather the leadership and security establishments of the government of Iraq and that the precision in which these targets were bombed was due in a large part due to the information gathered by weapons inspectors. I know that Iraq has legitimate grievances regarding the past work of the weapons inspectors and for that reason has sought to keep inspectors from returning to Iraq.

But I also know that there will be no peaceful resolution of this current crisis unless Iraq allows the unconditional return of weapons inspectors.

I was asking much from the Iraqi government, but knew the consequences of their refusing to allow the return of inspectors would be disastrous. My time in the Marine Corps and as a weapons inspector had taught me that if you're going to raise a problem you need to accompany it with a solution. I knew getting Iraq to agree to the unconditional return of inspectors would be difficult. The key to overcoming any Iraqi intransigence lay in getting some sort of assurance that this time around the Security Council would be alert for abuses in the inspection regime. But given the near absolute control the United States enjoyed over the council and its self-policing mechanisms, I felt there needed to be an additional mechanism for increasing Iraqi confidence. I called this mechanism the "honest broker."

The "honest broker" concept grew out of a trip I made to Canada in June, 2002. I had been invited to Ottawa to give testimony before the Canadian International Relations Committee. In meetings with members of parliament afterward, I was challenged to come up with the means to create a confidence-building mechanism that would not only allow

Iraq to have trust in the inspectors, but also the international community to have the same confidence in Iraq. Given the history of broken relations and mistrust between the two entities, who could be trusted if either side cried wolf? The idea was to create an impartial, objective observer group to monitor, not control, the interaction between inspector and inspected, making sure both parties abided by their obligations—the Iraqis to provide immediate, unrestricted access to sites designated for inspection, and the inspectors to stay within the mandate of their disarmament task, and not operate as a front for U.S. intelligence as they had in the past. I had raised the possibility, both in Ottawa and with the Canadian Ambassador to the United Nations in New York, about Canada playing a role in such an undertaking, and the Canadians had received the idea warmly.

One of the Canada's points of hesitation, though, was in going it alone, so while in South Africa I took the opportunity to meet with the Deputy Foreign Minister and key staff members from the South African Foreign Ministry to discuss the "honest broker" idea and the possibility of South African participation. The response was favorable, but I knew that something as controversial as this sometimes needed a little shove to get started. I had made the decision to take advantage of my global stage to provide the nudge.

"Iraq needs to know," I said to the Iraqi National Assembly, "that it is not alone in understanding that the concept of weapons inspections has been marred by the abuses of the past. Many in the international community understand that Iraq suffered from the abuse of the Security Council's mandate regarding inspections in the past and that under the current situation in which Iraq finds itself threatened by attack, the Iraqi government would not readily accede to any situation that permitted such inspections to return to work inside Iraq only to have this mandate again abused." I continued:

> There are those who in the near future will be addressing the issue of unconditional return of weapons inspectors to Iraq. They will seek to establish deadlines and issue ultimatums and threaten to use force to compel Iraq to let the inspectors return. What those who will make such proposals need to know is that such demands are in and of themselves conditional, and would only fuel the concerns inside Iraq over the abuses of the past. Such proposals are therefore doomed to fail, which in fact might be the very objective of those who would be making them, given that war is apparently their final objective, not disarmament or peace.

> There needs to be a way to push the issue of the return of weapons inspectors forward in a manner that at once allows for their unconditional return and yet provides assurances to Iraq that unfettered access will only be applied to disarmament issues, and not used to infringe on Iraq's sovereignty, dignity, and national security.

> There needs to be a confidence-building mechanism that allows for the monitoring of the interaction between weapons inspectors and Iraq to ensure that there are no deviations from the mandate of disarmament by the inspectors, as well as no obstruction of the work of the inspectors by Iraq.

> In the past few years, I've traveled extensively in the United States and around the world speaking about Iraq and the need for a resolution to the crisis over weapons inspectors.

Based on these travels, I believe that there is a way to provide such a confidence-building mechanism.

I call such a mechanism that of the honest broker—an independent, objective outside observer who monitors the work of the weapons inspectors and Iraq in fulfillment of the Security Council's disarmament mandate without interfering in the conduct of such work.

In order to have credibility in Iraq, and to avoid any perceptions of pressure from the Security Council or its members, such an honest broker would have to come from outside the United Nations framework, composed of a nation or a group of nations who embrace the framework of international law as set forth in the United Nations Charter and who are willing to place the credibility of their nation on the line in the performance of this monitoring function.

I've spoken with the representatives of several countries about this concept and they have indicated a willingness to step forward and work with Iraq and the Secretary General of the United Nations to serve as such an honest broker. All that is needed is for Iraq to agree to the unconditional return of inspectors in accordance with Security Council resolutions. The honest broker mechanism is not a precondition for inspections but rather a condition that will facilitate inspections. The honest broker mechanism allows for the rapid reintroduction of weapons inspectors into Iraq in a manner that would assure Iraq that the sins of the past would not be repeated.

The honest broker mechanism allows for the situation to be developed to facilitate a rapid finding of compliance on the part of Iraq regarding its disarmament obligations. In short, the honest broker mechanism allows for the peaceful, nonviolent resolution of the current stand-off between the United Nations and Iraq in full accordance with the letter of international law. If allowed to work, the honest broker mechanism can stop a war.

If allowed to work, the honest broker mechanism can lead to the lifting of economic sanctions against Iraq, returning to Iraq control of its economic resources so that it can proceed to reconstitute not weapons of mass destruction but rather its own economy and social fabric that has been torn asunder these many years. Once Iraq has been certified as being disarmed in accordance with the will of the Security Council, then the way could be cleared for the day in the near future when Iraq is once again welcomed back into the fold of international community in control of its own airspace and sovereign territory, ruled by a government of its own choosing.

"This will not be an easy task," I noted, aware of the obvious understatement, "and indeed the road towards the fulfillment of this goal is fraught with danger and difficulty. There are those who wish Iraq harm," I said, pointing a finger squarely at the Bush administration, "regardless of the circumstances or costs, and many of these currently reside in the government of the United States." I was speaking again to the American people, reaching out to them in an effort to assist them in breaking free from the chains of rhetorical tyranny they were being bound in.

"However, I ask of you to keep in mind what I have shared with you regarding the people of the United States and their relationship with the American government. Once the politics of fear can be defeated by the forces of truth then the current policies of the United States can be replaced by those that reject confrontation and embrace reconciliation and peaceful coexistence. Have confidence in the American people and the strength of American democracy. I know I do, which is the only reason why I am here before you today."

On September 16, scarcely a week after I delivered my presentation to the Iraqi National Assembly and impressed upon the Iraqi Government about the need for Iraq to open its doors unconditionally to the return of weapons inspectors, I was sitting in the green room on the set of CNN's *Crossfire*, waiting the signal to go on. A producer came up to me. "You may want to turn on the television," she said. I did so (to CNN, of course), and there was John King, reporting live, about the delivery by Iraq of a letter proclaiming its willingness to allow the return of U.N. weapons inspectors. The letter, delivered to U.N. Secretary General Kofi Annan, declared that Iraq would "allow the return of the United Nations weapons inspectors to Iraq without conditions." Iraq, the letter stated, made this decision to facilitate "the implementation of the relevant Security Council resolutions and to remove any doubts that Iraq still possesses weapons of mass destruction."

I was overcome by a wave of complete and utter relief. I had been preparing to go before Robert Novak and Paul Begala, the hosts of this evening's *Crossfire* segment, having to defend my recent actions. Instead, I was totally vindicated. The direction of questioning was about to dramatically shift, together with the message I wanted to deliver to the American people. Robert Novak got the ball rolling with his opening query: "CNN has reported that the administration is dismissive of this agreement by Iraq. In fact, as you're well aware, Secretary Rumsfeld, Vice President Cheney said they will never agree to open inspection. Do you believe that this administration is determined to let the bombing begin, no matter what the Iraqis do?"

I jumped on the opening provided. "Well, this is the ultimate challenge here. What is the policy of the United States? Is it disarmament? I mean, we've been told that Iraq represents a grave and imminent threat to our national security, worthy of war, worthy of the sacrifice of American service members' lives—the ultimate sacrifice somebody can give to their country. We're told that Iraq is this threat. And this threat comes from weapons of mass destruction."

This was almost too easy. "And now we have a situation where Iraq says what the United States said they had to say all along: unconditional return of inspectors with unfettered access. Is the issue weapons of mass destruction or disarmament? Then get the inspectors back in and let them do their job. And if Saddam fumbles, if he doesn't allow this to happen, now you have a case for war."

"Or," I asked, "is this really about regime removal? Is the number one policy objective of the Bush administration regime removal and all this talk about weapons of mass destruction nothing but a facade to legitimatize a war?"

It was Paul Begala's turn. "The White House story that John King broke on our network lists several other things. They say it's not just about weapons of mass destruction. They point out—this is quoting a White House official—there are resolutions dealing with repression within Iraq, resolutions with promises to make reparations to Kuwait, reparations dealing with unaccounted military personnel, including an American pilot. Now what about those three things? Iraq is clearly not going to comply with all that."

"And none of those," I retorted, "are worthy of a single American life being lost, with the exception of the American pilot. The concept of America going to war because Iraq owes Kuwait money is laughable. The concept of America going to war because Iraq is violating any number—one—of international agreements is laughable. We can only go to war when there is a threat to the national existence of the United States of America. Our national security must be at risk. And the only thing that Iraq has that could represent that kind of risk is weapons of mass destruction. And that's why we need to be focused on what the international community and international law has said all along: Iraq must disarm. There is absolutely no Security Council resolution on the book talking about the removal of Saddam Hussein from power. That is unilateral American policy."

I had done my part to expose the utter hypocrisy of the Bush administration's position on Iraq. This wasn't about weapons of mass destruction, or the threat posed by Iraq. This was about a naked grab for power. Surely the American people, and their elected representatives, would be able to see through the wall of lies and distortions of truth assembled by the president and his advisers. Now that Iraq had accepted the unconditional return of U.N. weapons inspectors, the issue of there being a threat to the United States worthy of our nation embarking on the path of war could no longer be sustained. A path towards peace had been opened up, and surely the people of America, and the world, would take advantage of it. So I believed.

Six months later my country found itself at war with Iraq. Why had we collectively chosen not to take the path of peace when proffered, deciding instead to stumble down the road to war? What was it that stymied any willingness on our part as a nation to seek truth, and instead encouraged our collective embrace of falsehoods? To avoid stepping over the dark precipice we find ourselves standing before, we must first be willing to answer these questions. Fortunately, the answers are there to be found, but finding them will require a level of introspection with which most Americans are uncomfortable—and unfamiliar. It is a journey most Americans are loath to take, but one which all Americans must take if we are to emerge from this period in our history intact as a people at one with their founding ideals and values, as a nation respectful of the rule of law, domestic and international alike, and not practitioners of the kind of crude vigilante justice that ruled us when we were still living on the frontier between civilized society and the wilderness.

Chapter Three Framing the Big Lie: The Birth of the PNAC Posse

"The great masses of the people will more easily fall
victim to a big lie than to a small one."
—Adolf Hitler

The old world definition of "frontier" was of a border town, a fortress, located in an uncertain or undeveloped region. It implied a semblance of order, the last bastion of civilization. The accepted American definition has added a new twist, "the farthest point of a settled country, where the wilds begin." The American definition implies a mixing of civilized and uncivilized worlds, an unsettled situation, an environment where the norms of the rule of law may not be fully applicable out of the sheer need for survival. The concepts of just conduct or fair dealings may, by necessity, have to be altered to fit the conditions of the moment. The administration of law through trial and due process would, in a frontier setting, be adapted to deal with that most pragmatic, basic need emanating from the law of nature—the need to survive. The complexities of the rules and regulations inherent in a society ruled by a system of laws representing so many shades of grey are anathema to the black and white realities and do or die mentality of the frontier. "Frontier justice," by extension, represents a fundamental simplification of the rule of law, recognizing and adapting to the extenuating circumstance of a dangerous world. But justice, frontier or otherwise, still requires us to maintain that which is right and just. There is an implied sense of honor and truth.

On March 19, 2003, the president of the United States, George W. Bush, ordered American military forces to engage in combat operations against the nation of Iraq. "Our nation enters this conflict reluctantly," the president said, steely-eyed and resolute, "yet our purpose is sure. The people of the United States and our friends and allies will not live at the mercy of an outlaw regime that threatens the peace with weapons of mass murder." The president could very well have been a frontier sheriff, explaining to the assembled town folk why he was taking their men out on a posse, to hunt down a dangerous criminal element. The "outlaw" regime of Saddam Hussein was threatening the edges of civilized society, and the frontier was at risk. Justice needed to be served, frontier justice, through a war ostensibly waged to preserve democracy and the American way of life from the threat of an outlaw regime possessing illegal weapons of mass destruction. But what happens if it turns out—as it now appears to be the case—that there was no such threat, that Iraq in fact had no such weapons, that the war waged by the United States against Iraq had no basis in legitimacy? Would justice—frontier or otherwise—have been served?

The entire Bush administration case rests on there being weapons of mass destruction in Iraq in violation of United Nations Security Council resolutions. This was the president's message, one he had repeatedly presented to the American people in the buildup to war. An illuminating example of this was the president's statement of October 7, 2002, on the eve of the congressional vote to grant the president the authority to wage war on Iraq. "The danger is already significant," the president warned, "and it only grows worse with time. If we know Saddam Hussein has dangerous weapons today—and we do—does it make any sense for the world to wait to confront him as he grows even stronger and develops even more dangerous weapons?" The president continued:

> We know that the regime has produced thousands of tons of chemical agents, including mustard gas, sarin nerve gas, VX nerve gas . . . every chemical and biological weapon that Iraq has or makes is a direct violation of the truce that ended the Persian Gulf War in 1991. Yet, Saddam Hussein has chosen to build and keep these weapons despite international sanctions, U.N. demands, and isolation from the civilized world.

Such a statement, dripping in detail, echoed similar points repeated over and over again by the president and his advisors when drumming up the case for war: chemical and biological agents, missiles, nuclear weapons, covert concealment, deception . . . danger.

To the American people the Bush administration played the threat of Iraqi weapons of mass destruction like a terrible puzzle, a modern-day Gordian knot that could only be solved by a decisive stroke of the American sword. It was a puzzle that couldn't be solved in accordance with the rules, because (according to the Bush administration policy framers) the Iraqi regime refused to play by the rules. It was a real threat, and yet it could not be physically identified because of the deception of Saddam Hussein. It was a giant algorithm, threatening to engulf the world, for which there was no theorem to aid in finding the solution.

But we now have the theorem needed to solve this problem. We now know that there are no weapons of mass destruction in Iraq. We now know that Iraq had, in fact, disarmed, and was not pursuing programs to develop weapons of mass destruction. When this theorem is applied to all that has been said by the Bush administration, it then appears that the only willful charade was that being carried out by president Bush on the American people, the Congress of the United States, and the world.

The intelligence cited by the president has turned out to be either egregiously erroneous or simply pulled from thin air. The details so precisely set forth have turned out to be void of any substance. Did the president lie, or was the intelligence fundamentally flawed? Either case is disturbing. Either case is damning. And either case underscores the fact that, in America's war with Iraq, it was the Bush administration, and not Saddam Hussein, who engaged in actions of systematic defiance of the world.

This was not justice, not even frontier justice, but rather a gross perversion of justice. What was perpetrated by the

United States in Iraq was a moral ambush on the values and ideals of American society, a bushwhacking of international law carried out by a president who lost touch with what it means to have the honor of leading the United States of America. Traditional frontier justice, even vigilante style, has a sense of honor attached, as those who perpetrate any given act are up front about what it is they are trying to accomplish. Bushwhacking is a moral coward's way of doing business, where an act is carried out behind a wall of deception. President Bush and his team of bushwhackers hid their true objectives from the American people behind an elaborately constructed wall of fear and ignorance. Each brick of this wall was a carefully crafted lie pertaining to "threats" to the security of the American people and the American way of life. And for the most part the American people, together with their elected officials in Congress and the supposed "watch dogs" of democracy, the fourth estate, bought the lies without question, ignoring the fact that this wall wasn't designed to shield them from lurking threats, but from the truth that the greatest threat to the security of the American people actually lay with those who were building the wall—the Bush administration.

The key to this whole deception is the Big Lie: Iraq had weapons of mass destruction which it maintained in defiance of international law, and it refused to abide by its obligations to be disarmed of such weapons. We now know this not to be true. The Big Lie has been exposed. But what good is exposing the lie if there will be no consequences for those who gave birth to the lie, nurtured the lie, and unleashed the lie on the American people and the world? The ramifications of the Big Lie are many, not least of which is the frontal assault it launches on the very principles of law, order, and doing that which is right and just. The Big Lie does away with traditional forms of justice, replacing them with the expediency of frontier justice. But the Big Lie goes further, eroding even the simplistic structures of frontier justice to the point that bushwhacking—an ambush carried out behind a shield of deceit—is recognized as an acceptable means of resolving issues of grave importance. In this manner, Team Bush and the Big Lie have successfully bushwhacked the two institutions, international law and American democracy, that stood in the way of their march to absolute power.

International law is the framework that holds the international community together as a cohesive, interactive entity. The key to this is a unified set of principles and values which serve as a common guide for all to follow. In the post-World War II environment these principles and values have been codified within the Charter of the United Nations. While far from perfect, the rules and regulations set forth in the charter have succeeded in helping the global community navigate some seriously troubled waters during the five decades the charter has been in place, avoiding the kind of global conflagration from which it was born. The charter is useful only so far as its collective membership finds it useful. But Sheriff Bush and his band of bushwhackers, instituting their own perverse brand of frontier justice, found the charter to be an impediment to their larger ambition of global domination in the same way a west Texas lynch mob would find a traveling circuit judge an impediment to their ambitions to string up a sheep herder falsely accused of being a cattle rustler in order to gain control over the sheep herder's grazing rights.

The solution? Destroy confidence in the efficacy of international law by ignoring the very institution that mandated the disarmament of Iraq—the United Nations Security Council—denigrating it by proclaiming it unable, or unwilling, to enforce its own laws regarding the disarmament of Iraq. The Big Lie. Iraq has weapons of mass destruction. Witness Sheriff Bush's speech to the United Nations General Assembly on September 12, 2002. Saddam Hussein, he said, "continues to develop weapons of mass destruction. The first time we may be completely certain he has a—nuclear weapons is when, God forbids [*sic*], he uses one. We owe it to all our citizens to do everything in our power to prevent that day from coming." Sheriff Bush went even further, chiding the world's assembled diplomats:

> The conduct of the Iraqi regime is a threat to the authority of the United Nations, and a threat to peace. Iraq has answered a decade of U.N. demands with a decade of defiance. All the world now faces a test, and the United Nations a difficult and defining moment. Are Security Council resolutions to be honored and enforced, or cast aside without consequence? Will the United Nations serve the purpose of its founding, or will it be irrelevant?

But what Sheriff Bush didn't say, and what we now know, is that, on the issue of Iraqi weapons of mass destruction, the world had already faced up to its test: Iraq had in fact been disarmed. Saddam Hussein was not continuing to develop weapons of mass destruction. He had in fact eliminated these weapons. On that twelfth day of September 2002, the United

Nations was truly at a defining moment, not in terms of its willingness to come to grips with the Iraqi dictator, but rather how it would choose to respond to the bushwhacking practitioner of American frontier justice. We now know, in refusing to stand up to the demands of President Bush, the United Nations in fact failed to serve the purpose of its founding, and has allowed itself to become irrelevant, which of course was the objective of Team Bush all along. Will the world body recover from the damage inflicted by the actions of the American bushwhackers, or will it complete its slide into irrelevance and obscurity by acceding to every demand made by the new global hegemonists in Washington, DC?

American democracy? You can't have democracy without the bond of truth that exists between the people and those whom they elect to represent them. If that bond is broken, then there must be an accounting to restore faith in the system. Yet Team Bush continues to perpetrate the Big Lie to the American people, and even though the lie has been laid bare, there is no outrage. The United States seems to have been stricken by a collective case of "Stockholm Syndrome," where having been kidnaped by President Bush and his team of neo-conservative ideologues, we have adapted to their message even though in our heart we know it to be fundamentally at odds with what we as a people stand for.

Is this the end, then, of American democracy as envisioned by those who framed the Constitution over two hundred and twenty years ago, or is this passivity a result of ignorance, a lack of understanding of the Big Lie and the dangers it hides? The former forecasts the death of the American dream, a nation of ideals and values which inspired a free and independent people to do great things over the course of the past two centuries. The latter inspires hope that, once exposed to the truth about the Big Lie, the American people will cleanse themselves of this contamination and restore the American democratic republic to its proper course of historical development. There will be an accounting—there *must* be an accounting—if we are to survive as the nation we envision ourselves to be, a nation of laws as set forth by the Constitution of the United States of America. But before we can vanquish those who sell the Big Lie, we must first deconstruct the Big Lie as it pertains to Iraqi weapons of mass destruction.

Where to begin? For every journey, especially a journey of truth, there must be a beginning. The Big Lie that Team Bush told to the American people was an inherited lie. It did not begin with the administration of George W. Bush, our forty-third president, but rather with his father, George Herbert Walker Bush, the forty-first president. And, paradoxically, when the Big Lie was born, it wasn't even a lie. It was the truth.

"As today's resolution states," the younger President Bush said in October 2002, referring to the recently passed Security Council resolution 1441, "Iraq is already in material breach of past U.N. demands. Iraq has aggressively pursued weapons of mass destruction, even while inspectors were inside the country. Iraq has undermined the effectiveness of weapons inspectors with ploys, delays, and threats, making their work impossible and leading to four years of no inspections at all."

If that statement had been made in July 1991, by Bush the forty-first, it would have been dead-on accurate. At that time, the United Nations Security Council had just confronted Iraq over its efforts to deceive U.N. weapons inspectors by hiding critical aspects of its nuclear weapons program. The Security Council had just passed a new resolution, 707 (1991), designed to deal with Iraq's actions. How so? By authorizing military action to enforce the will of the council? No. By demanding, once again, that Iraq fully comply with its obligation to disarm, re-submit a full, final, and complete declaration of its entire holdings of weapons of mass destruction, and fully cooperate with the mandated tasks of the inspectors. The council sent the inspectors back into Iraq.

"Iraq has generally engaged in obfuscation and evasion of its obligations," the elder Bush wrote in a letter to Congress on July 16, 1991. "In recent weeks, public attention has focused on Iraq's nuclear equipment and material, but this has also been true with respect to Iraq's undeclared chemical weapons and ballistic missiles and its continuing refusal to acknowledge any biological weapons development activities. We will not allow these Iraqi actions to succeed."

What was George Herbert Walker Bush's grand strategy to thwart the dictator Saddam? Invasion? No. "We will continue to insist on the full identification and complete elimination of all relevant items as well as the imposition of a thorough and effective monitoring regime to assure Iraq's long-term compliance with Resolution 687."

Why, when the Big Lie was in fact the Whole Truth, did the first Bush undertake a different course of action than his prodigal son? The answer: Because at that time the agenda was different. The elder Bush was operating under a different set of marching orders which reflected a respect for international law and the institutions involved. Explaining why he did not order U.S.-led forces into Baghdad to remove Saddam Hussein from power after the first U.S. war with Iraq, back in 1991, the elder Bush noted:

> We had been self-consciously trying to set a pattern for hand-ling aggression in the post-Cold War world. Going in and occupying Iraq, thus unilaterally exceeding the United Nation's mandate, would have destroyed the precedent of international response to aggression that we hoped to estab-lish. Had we gone the invasion route, the United States could conceivably still be an occupying power in a bitterly hostile land.[1]

James Baker, secretary of state under the first Bush, punctuat-ed the importance that administration placed on United Nations-based coalitions in furthering the American nation-al interest, saying that at the time (1991):

> We were leery of fragmenting Iraq or dissolving the coalition. We needed the coalition as much in the postwar period as we had before the war . . . we had learned that Saddam Hussein's program to develop weapons of mass destruction was both more substantial and better concealed than we believed at the outset. We were determined to use our victory in Desert Storm to put the Iraqi regime under the intense glare of the most intrusive weapons-inspections regime ever developed, to root out every last bit of that program . . . we needed imple-mentation of existing U.N. resolutions (and an additional U.N. resolution enacted), and we needed all our coalition partners to be with us to achieve this.[2]

But perhaps it takes Colin Powell, the elder President Bush chairman of the joint chiefs of staff and the only prominent policy formulator other than Dick Cheney to transition from the administration of Bush the forty-first president to Bush forty-third, to best put into perspective the decision not to remove Saddam Hussein from power, either as a result of Operation Desert Storm, or in its aftermath, as a consequence of noncompliance with U.N.-mandated disarmament. Powell, writing in 1995, underscored the importance of a strong Iraq, even one ruled by Saddam Hussein, to American national security interests. "Our practical intention," Powell wrote, "was to leave Baghdad enough power to survive as a threat to an Iran that remained bitterly hostile towards the United States . . . it would not contribute to the stability we want in the Middle East to have Iraq fragmented into separate Sunni, Shi'a, and Kurd political entities."[3] This, of course, could not be achieved by throttling Saddam every time he stepped over the boundaries established by the United Nations.

Adherence to the rule of law and maintenance of stability in a region of vital strategic importance—two admirable goals, implemented under conditions calling for admirable constraint. How did the American foreign policy ship drift so far off course in the decade separating the two Iraqi conflicts? The answer lies not in the success of the first Bush administration to set sound policy, but rather the failure of that same administration to adhere to this policy.

If one were to list that administration's top three policy priorities regarding Iraq as they existed in July 1991, they would have been maintenance of stability and security, main-

tenance of an effective and viable coalition, and implementation of an effective disarmament regime. Saddam Hussein
had been marginalized, and while his continued existence
would be tolerated as a means of maintaining stability inside
Iraq, no one in Washington, DC took either Saddam or his
regime seriously.

By October 1992, on the eve of presidential elections, the
top three priorities had changed dramatically, to the containment of Saddam Hussein, destabilization of Saddam Hussein,
and regime removal in Iraq. Regional stability and security
remained a concern, but only as a tangent to the new principle focus on Saddam Hussein. What prompted this shift?
Domestic politics. The administration of George H. W. Bush
may have won the war with Iraq in 1991, but by 1992 it had,
in the minds of most Americans, lost the peace. This perception was creating a serious domestic political issue for a president whose main strength as a candidate was the perception
of his administration standing tall against Saddam Hussein,
and domestic politics trump noble concepts about rule of law
and international stability every time.

Why did the peace seem lost? Because Bush the Elder had
not promised the American people containment and stability
when he mobilized the youth of America for war with Iraq in
1990 and 1991, but rather a decisive confrontation with the
forces of evil personified by Saddam Hussein and his regime.
As explained to the American people, Saddam Hussein was
"evil," a threat every bit as dangerous and nefarious as Adolf
Hitler. Of course, once you invoke the name of Hitler, especially in analogous form, there is no room for compromise,
for backing down, for anything less than decisive confronta-

tion, lest you invoke similar visions of Neville Chamberlain and Munich in 1938.

Saddam was, after all, a man who "systematically raped, pillaged, and plundered a tiny nation [*i.e.*, Kuwait], no threat to his own," the first Bush said in his address to the American people on January 16, 1991, announcing the start of Operation Desert Storm. "He [Saddam] subjected the people of Kuwait to unspeakable atrocities—and among those maimed and murdered, innocent children . . . the terrible crimes and tortures committed by Saddam's henchmen against the innocent people of Kuwait are an affront to mankind and a challenge to the freedom of all."

Bush the Elder had played the Saddam-as-evil card extensively in the lead up to the 1990 midterm elections, politicizing an extremely sensitive subject—war. In campaign stops across the country—places like Burlington, Stamford, Albuquerque, Dallas, Mashpee, Arlington, and Honolulu (using Pearl Harbor as the thematic backdrop), Bush pounded home the central theme of good versus evil. "Today in the Persian Gulf," he said on October 28, 1990, "the world is once again faced with the challenge of perfect clarity. Saddam Hussein has given us a whole plateful of clarity, because today, in the Persian Gulf, what we are looking at is good and evil, right and wrong."

This struggle against evil, according to Bush, was not trivial, but fundamental in nature. "We're dealing with Hitler revisited," the president reminded his audience earlier, on October 23, 1990, "a totalitarianism and a brutality that is naked and unprecedented in modern times. And that must not stand. We cannot talk about compromise when you have that kind of behavior going on this very minute."

No compromise, meaning that there must be an accounting. "When this ordeal is over," the president said on that same date, "and when Kuwait is once again a sovereign and free member of the family of nations, Saddam Hussein must pay for the pain and the hardship that he has caused. The world will hold him accountable, just as it held Adolph Hitler accountable in the wake of the destruction of World War II."

By August 25, 1992, the president's message had changed dramatically. "Instead of playing the world's policeman," he said, "we worked with the United Nations to destroy Iraq's remaining weapons of mass destruction, to keep Iraq under control. Through an embargo, through tight control over oil exports and U.N. inspections, we are putting the lid on Saddam. And believe me, he is going to live up to each and every one of those U.N. resolutions. I am determined to see that, and I will." Resolute? Yes. But maintaining an embargo and having tight control over Iraqi oil exports was a far cry from the harsh retribution the president alluded to back in the fall of 1990. The crimes of Saddam Hussein, Bush the Elder announced on October 28, 1990, "are punishable under the principles adopted by the allies in 1945 and unanimously reaffirmed by the United Nations in 1950. Two weeks ago I made mention of the Nuremberg trials. Saddam Hussein must know the stakes are high."

But as the 1992 presidential election loomed, Saddam Hussein remained entrenched in power in Baghdad, and President Bush was doing his best to spin public perception about the lost peace in his favor. "It was never an objective of the United Nations under these many resolutions—twelve resolutions—to get him out of office," the president explained in July, 1992. "The resolution was to get him out of Kuwait . . .

we were fantastically successful there." And while he openly mocked those who favored giving continued economic sanctions a try prior to his January 16, 1991 decision to go to war ("I keep going back to the 'let sanctions work'—do you remember that cry?" Bush crowed during the presidential debate of October 21, 1992. "If we had let sanctions work back there, we would have had the coalition fall apart and the main objective would have been totally unmet."), the president's only solution for dealing with Saddam Hussein in 1992 was continued sanctions. "The regime of Saddam Hussein continues to pose an unusual and extraordinary threat to the national security and foreign policy of the United States, as well as to regional peace and security," the president wrote in a report to Congress dated August 3, 1992. "The United States will therefore continue to apply *economic sanctions* (italics added) to deter Iraq from threatening peace and stability in the region."

So much for "Nuremberg-like" retribution. The American public had been conditioned to view Iraq in stark "good versus evil" terms. A nation of over twenty million persons had been reduced to but one: Saddam Hussein. And, thanks to the exaggerated posturing of the elder Bush, the American people likened Saddam Hussein to Adolph Hitler. This created a mind set of uncompromising "black versus white" moral certainty regarding a problem that instead required enlightened awareness concerning the complexities involved in navigating a course defined by the reality that the world is not black and white, but in fact so many shades of grey.

In November 1992 Bush the Elder lost his bid for re-election and was replaced by Arkansas Governor Bill Clinton, a man not noted for his depth of expertise on matters pertaining to international affairs. Many in the Bush Defense Department wanted to pressure Clinton into sustaining a strong stance against Iraq, and sought to ratchet up the pressure accordingly. On January 15 and 16 the soon-to-be former President Bush ordered a series of attacks against targets in Iraq, ostensibly in response to Iraqi acts of defiance toward the establishment of a so-called no-fly zone in southern Iraq similar to the one in place over northern Iraq since 1991. The Iraqi government mistakenly believed it could pressure the newly elected president to change course regarding U.S.-Iraq policy by creating a confrontation. Iraq was refusing to allow U.N. logistics aircraft to enter into Iraqi airspace covered by the southern no-fly zone, saying it could not guarantee the safety of the aircraft or its crew. This had the effect of stymieing weapons inspections, since many of the inspection personnel ended up stranded outside the borders of Iraq. In addition, Iraq reinforced its air defense posture, which included firing on U.S. and British aircraft operating in the no-fly zones. President Bush ordered a series of air strikes in response. "Let's just hope that Saddam Hussein got the message," the president said, hoping Bill Clinton was watching, and listening, as well. "I hope that he will comply with these United Nations resolutions."

On January 17, three days before leaving office, Bush followed up these strikes with a massive cruise missile attack on Iraqi factories in southern Baghdad, which was of interest to U.N. weapons inspectors because of the facilities' past involvement in nuclear weapons related activity. A signal was clearly being sent—but to whom? President-elect Bill Clinton certainly got the point. "Saddam Hussein," he said in commenting on the strikes, "should be very clear in understanding that the current and the next administration are in complete agreement on the necessity of his fully complying with all relevant United Nations Security Council resolutions."

The new president then made it clear, both in his actions and his words, that he would maintain the policy of containment he inherited from Bush. On January 21, one day after he took his oath of office, President Clinton ordered U.S. warplanes to bomb Iraqi air defense sites in northern Iraq that threatened allied crews patrolling the no-fly zone. A similar strike took place the next day. "It is the American policy," he said on January 26, 1993, "and that is what we are going to stay with."

Iraq eventually backed down and allowed U.N. aircraft to resume operations inside Iraq. Clinton authorized continued air strikes in the no-fly zones on an intermittent basis throughout 1993 in response to ongoing acts of Iraqi defiance, and in June 1993 launched his own cruise missile attack against Baghdad, striking the Iraqi Intelligence Service's headquarters after linking Iraqi agents with an alleged assassination attempt on the elder Bush in Kuwait.

Clinton had inherited from Bush a policy of containment, but containment without an endgame strategy wasn't policy—it was the antithesis of policy. While President Bush the Elder had announced his desire to see Saddam Hussein removed from power (and in fact had signed a "lethal finding" authorizing the CIA to take actions to that effect), the program of regime removal never got off the ground. The Clinton administration had inherited this presidential "lethal finding" from President Bush, which authorized the CIA to create conditions inside Iraq which would result in the elimination of Saddam Hussein. To implement this policy, the CIA had formed an operational entity known as the Iraqi Operations Group, or IOG.

The IOG was struggling to find its purpose during the first Bush administration, and in the opening months of the Clinton administration was consigned to carrying out simple propaganda-style operations (such as funding propaganda radio broadcasts) that had no real chance of success with regards to regime change in Baghdad. The radio broadcasts were conducted in ostensible support of an Iraqi opposition organization known as the Iraqi National Congress (INC), a loose umbrella group of Iraqi expatriates opposed to Saddam Hussein who came together in late 1991 under the leadership of a charismatic, yet controversial, former Iraqi banker named Achmed Chalabi. In 1992 Chalabi and the INC began receiving direct funding support from the IOG, and by 1993 Chalabi had opened offices inside Kurdish safe havens in northern Iraq operating under the umbrella of American and British air power. But the INC was not a serious threat to the regime of Saddam Hussein.

The CIA's efforts were never seen by the Clinton administration as a stand alone solution to the Iraq problem. Instead, they were rolled into a new, evolving policy of "dual containment," which addressed U.S. strategic interests in the Persian Gulf by combining the threats posed by unfriendly regimes in Iran and Iraq as a singular problem, both of which would be contained in a manner that restricted their respective military ambitions in the region. But "dual containment" was a sloppy policy, full of inconsistencies brought on by the fact that many of the assumptions which held the policy together conceptually were, in fact, wrong (for example, the coalition assembled by the first President Bush in 1991 was, by 1994, no longer the viable, single-minded entity, with the French, Russians and Chinese splintering off in their own separate directions).

Up through the end of 1994, the Clinton administration had been conducting a fairly reactive policy toward Iraq, allowing the combined efforts of U.N. weapons inspections, economic sanctions, and enforcement of the two no-fly zones over Iraq to contain Baghdad. This policy was altered only when Iraq attempted to break out of this containment, as witnessed by the Iraqi military movements toward Kuwait and the subsequent U.S. counter-deployments in October 1994. The resulting crisis severely strained the postwar coalition, exposing serious fractures on issues not just pertaining to the American military buildup, but the viability of economic sanctions and even the U.N. weapons inspection regime. This crisis led policy makers in Washington to focus on the possibility of a resurgent Iraq, an Iraq free of economic sanctions and intrusive weapons inspections, and the long-term costs associated with such a turn of events, and a decision was taken to seek, in a concerted fashion, the removal of Saddam Hussein from power through covert action. "Dual containment' may have been the name of the policy, but the name of the game became "regime removal."

The CIA, through the IOG, felt that it could engage in the kind of lengthy salami tactics that had proven so effective in Afghanistan against the then-Soviet Union, slicing away at Saddam's sphere of control until he could claim only

Baghdad and his hometown of Tikrit as being under his direct sphere of influence. Weapons inspections and economic sanctions played into this, as did the establishment and enforcement of the no-fly zones. But there needed to be something more—an operational arm.

In October 1994, following Saddam's Kuwait adventure, the IOG established a full-time clandestine operations station in Salahuddin, an INC-controlled town in northern Iraq. The goal of the IOG was to gradually build up the military capabilities of the INC and their Kurdish allies, and drive Saddam's forces from northern Iraq altogether. These plans were put in place prior to the Iraqi move on Kuwait, and were representative of a long-term approach to solving the Saddam problem.

The Iraqi move on Kuwait in October 1994, and the resultant American military buildup, exposed the fragile political realities associated with the Clinton policy of containment. The massive military deployment into Kuwait and the Persian Gulf was executed at great cost, both in terms of fiscal expense and, to an even greater extent, operational readiness of the military forces involved (the deployment interfered with training and troop rotation schedules, adversely affecting personnel management without resolving the root cause of the disruption—the situation vis-à-vis Iraq). The Clinton team was already receiving a large amount of criticism for its defense policies, and the large-scale deployment of military resources to the Persian Gulf in October 1994 strained the Pentagon's resources across the board. When diplomatic intervention by Russia forestalled military action, many in the Department of Defense let it be known that the U.S. military could not afford to get caught up in a game of "yo-yo" with Iraq, responding with expensive yet indecisive military deployments every time the Iraqi dictator decided to flex his muscles. Iraq was again becoming a domestic political liability. Clinton could not be blamed for failing to oust the Iraqi dictator in 1991—that remained the first Bush's sin—but he could be blamed for looking less than resolute in the face of Iraqi defiance. There was no longer patience in the White House for the kind of long-term strategy of attrition being pursued by the IOG in its support of the INC. A new strategy was needed, together with a new cast of characters.

The Iraqi Operatoins Group turned its attentions away from Achmed Chalabi's INC, and instead started supporting a new group of Iraqi expatriates known as the Iraqi National Alliance, or INA. The IOG committed considerable resources to what was referred to inside Washington as a "silver bullet" operation, a military coup to topple Saddam Hussein carried out by officers inside Saddam's vaunted Republican Guard and security establishments. An operation was planned for mid-June, 1996. However, it turned out that the INA had been infiltrated by agents of the Iraqi dictator, and the "silver bullet" coup collapsed in a wave of arrests and executions. Saddam followed up his success in rolling up the CIA's INA-based operation by doing the same to the now-marginalized INC, sending his tanks into Kurdistan and rousting the group, together with their CIA controllers, out of Iraq. The Clinton administration could do little more in response than throw a few cruise missiles at Iraqi targets in southern Iraq, far from the area of contention. A decision to further tighten the containment of Saddam by expanding the southern no-fly zone from the 32nd parallel to the 34th parallel only succeeded in fracturing an already strained coalition, prompting the French to drop out of the enforcement effort.

President Clinton had committed a major sin in the eyes of the Republican hawks that had populated the Defense Department during the presidency of the first Bush, and who were now festering in various think-tanks and similar repositories for out-of-work ideologues. Clinton had embarrassed the United States. Worse, he was undoing Bush's grand victory over Iraq by letting Saddam slip his neck out of the noose the Republican administration has managed to throw over him in 1991.

The Clinton administration's botched handling of foreign affairs, exemplified by the Iraqi case, threatened to undo everything the Republicans had achieved under Ronald Reagan and George H. W. Bush as far as winning the Cold War and creating a unipolar world in which the United States reigned supreme. Under the leadership of President Clinton—who was widely reviled in neoconservative circles as a draft dodger with low regard for the power of the United States—the great Republican victory was being squandered. "In this extraordinary new world," Clinton's national security advisor, Tony Lake, explained in the summer of 1993, "the greatest opportunities for our diplomacy involve multilateral action . . . that is why we are seeing an extraordinary increase now in the importance of the United Nations and in the importance specifically of United Nations peace-keeping operations, which we are now supporting . . . the United States must and will act unilaterally when it must," Mr. Lake noted, "but we are more and more interested in acting multi-laterally and in leading multilateral efforts to resolve our international problems."[4]

Such statements were blasphemy to true believers among the neoconservative ranks of the out-of-power Republicans. Under the Dick Cheney Pentagon of the first Bush, these hawks had found a home where they were free to stamp their brand of ideology on the formulation of the elder Bush's "New World Order." In early 1992 two of these neoconservative thinkers—Paul Wolfowitz and I. Lewis "Scooter" Libby, both working for Secretary of Defense Dick Cheney—drafted something known as the Defense Policy Document. It was a stunning declaration of unilateral American power, in effect a statement of intent regarding the establishment of an American empire.

"Our first objective," the draft document read, "is to prevent the re-emergence of a new rival. This . . . requires that we endeavor to prevent any hostile power from dominating a region whose resources would, under consolidated control, be sufficient to generate global power." To prevent this, therefore, America must dominate all regions. How? Simply, according to the drafters of this new ideology: "First the U.S. must show the leadership necessary to establish and protect a new order that holds the promise of convincing potential competitors that they need not aspire to a greater role or pursue a more aggressive posture to protect their legitimate interests." The framers of this new world order believed it was the role of the United States to "discourage" nations "from challenging our leadership or seeking to overturn the established political and economic order." The means of such discouragement? Mechanisms "for deterring potential competitors from even aspiring to a larger regional or global role." Translation? The United States takes advantage of the demise of the former Soviet Union to impose its unilateral domination of the globe in all matters political, economic, and military.

Leaked to the *New York Times* in early 1992 and roundly criticized in Congress as irresponsible (Delaware Senator Joe Biden blasted the document for its pre-emptive nature and the fact that it called for a "Pax Americana" that wouldn't work), the draft Defense Policy Guidance document was pulled back and extensively rewritten. In any case, the elder Bush lost his bid for re-election before any action could be taken to codify this new ideology. The neoconservative post-Cold War revolution was stymied. The thwarted revolutionaries, in intellectual exile, plotted their return to power.

It didn't take them long to exploit the fumbling Clinton administration. By 1997, the neoconservatives had regrouped into a "nonprofit educational organization" which believed that "American leadership is good both for America and for the world." Of course, such a truism came with a catch: "Such leadership," this non-profit organization stated, "requires military strength, diplomatic energy, and commitment to moral principle." Unfortunately for the American people (and the world, one would presume), "too few political leaders today are making the case for global leadership."[5] Shame on you, Bill Clinton.

The Project for a New American Century, or PNAC, as this "non-profit educational organization" came to be known, was the brain child of neoconservative guru William Kristol. In its "Statement of Foreign Policy Principles," published on

June 3, 1997, PNAC resurrected the global domination theme of the Wolfowitz-Libby Defense Policy Document. Asking the basic question, "Does the United States have the resolve to shape a new century favorable to American principles and interests?" and noting "the incoherent policies of the Clinton Administration," PNAC advocated "a military that is strong and ready to meet both present and future challenges; a foreign policy that boldly and purposefully promotes American principles abroad; and national leadership that accepts the United States' global responsibilities." The Project for a New American Century sought to remind all Americans of our collective need to "accept responsibility for America's unique role in preserving and extending an international order friendly to our security, our prosperity, and our principles," noting that "such a Reaganite policy of military strength and moral clarity may not be fashionable today. But it is necessary if the United States is to build on the successes of this past century and to ensure our security and our greatness in the next." Adding their names to this statement were notables such as former Secretary of Defense Dick Cheney, his disciples, Paul Wolfowitz and "Scooter' Libby, Reaganites Donald Rumsfeld, Elliott Abrams, Zalmay Khalilzad, Frank Gaffney, Dan Quayle, Fred Ikle, William Bennet, and a whole host of neoconservative ideologues. The PNAC "Statement of Principles" was nothing less than a declaration of war against the Clinton administration, a moralizing lynch-mob intent on re- asserting so-called Reaganite moral clarity to a new world order solely defined by the United States.

Iraq was the first victim of frontier justice, PNAC-style. On January 26, 1998, the PNAC posse sent a letter to Bill

Clinton setting out their vision of how American policy toward Iraq should unfold. "We are writing you," the posse announced, "because we are convinced that current American policy toward Iraq is not succeeding, and that we may soon face a threat in the Middle East more serious than any we have known since the end of the Cold War." The neo-conservative modern day vigilantes urged the president to enunciate a strategy that "would secure the interests of the U.S. and our friends and allies around the world" by seeking "the removal of Saddam Hussein's regime from power."

Why this new strategy? To eliminate "the possibility that Iraq will be able to use or threaten to use weapons of mass destruction." Clearly, this threat was more serious than the possibility of global extinction that the Cold War offered. Hyperbole and exaggeration were the strong suit of the PNAC posse. "We urge you to articulate this aim," they continued, "and to turn your administration's attention to implementing a strategy for removing Saddam's regime from power. This will require a full complement of diplomatic, political, and military efforts." And, of course, the PNAC posse, having articulated their vision of the American diplomatic, political, and military ideal, were only too ready to tell the president how to go forward. "We believe the U.S. has the authority under existing U.N. resolutions to take the necessary steps, including military steps, to protect our vital interests in the Gulf. In any case, American policy cannot continue to be crippled by a misguided insistence on unanimity in the U.N. Security Council."

Regime change disguised as disarmament was the name of the game. The fact that Iraq had, by this time, been fundamentally disarmed (as already stated, U.N. weapons inspectors were able to account for 90–95 percent of the proscribed weapons produced by Iraq), and that the totality of Iraq's capable industrial infrastructure was under the most comprehensive and intrusive on-site inspection regime in the history of arms control, meant nothing to a posse determined to hang someone as a way of demonstrating their determination to inflict their vision on the world. Nearly a decade of concerted effort by the United States to eliminate Saddam Hussein through covert action went unnoticed and unmentioned in circles trying to come to grips with Iraqi intransigence over the intrusive practices of U.N. weapons inspection teams that were literally crawling with CIA covert operatives. The truth mattered not at all, only the perception of a threat, and the need to eliminate this threat signified. Iraq was an all too convenient vehicle for selling the PNAC posse's world vision to America. And it worked.

On October 31, 1998, both houses of Congress, in bipartisan fashion, voted to approve Public Law 105-338, also known as the Iraq Liberation Act of 1998, Section 3 of which declared the "Sense of the Congress regarding United States policy toward Iraq" in that it should be the policy of the United States to support efforts to remove the regime headed by Saddam Hussein from power in Iraq and to promote the emergence of a democratic government to replace that regime." The principle vehicle for achieving this goal would be the Iraqi National Congress, or INC, under Ahmad Chalabi, last seen in 1996, fleeing Iraq together with their CIA controllers, the Iraqi Army hot on their heels.

The PNAC championing of Chalabi and the INC got a further boost during the 2000 presidential elections, when it was able to orchestrate the inclusion of language in the Republican Party platform that not only criticized President Clinton, but endorsed regime change in Iraq. "The administration," the platform read, "has pretended to support the removal of Saddam Hussein from power, but did nothing when Saddam Hussein's army smashed the democratic opposition in northern Iraq in August 1996. The administration also surrendered the diplomatic initiative to Iraq and Iraq's friends, and failed to champion the international inspectors charged with erasing Iraq's nuclear, biological, chemical, and ballistic missile programs." Saddam's forces massacred Iraqis who heeded the elder Bush's call for them to overthrow the dictator. Now the Republicans called for "a comprehensive plan for the removal of Saddam Hussein" which backed Ahmad Chalabi and the Iraqi National Congress, "an umbrella organization reflecting a broad and representative group of Iraqis who wish to free their country from the scourge of Saddam Hussein's regime."

And so in November 2000, the American people picked the candidate of the PNAC posse to the highest elected office of the land—president of the United States of America. Sheriff Bush put the dictator Saddam squarely on notice during his inaugural address on January 20, 2001: "We will confront weapons of mass destruction, so that a new century is spared new horrors. The enemies of liberty and our country should make no mistake: America remains engaged in the world by history and by choice, shaping a balance of power that favors freedom."

The newly-elected president, in that same address, alluded to Thomas Jefferson at the time of the signing of the Declaration of Independence in 1776, by declaring to the

American people, "And an angel still rides in the whirlwind and directs this storm." But this was 2000, not 1776, and the man speaking was a failed Texas oilman, not a patriotic American visionary. A new dawn was breaking, a new era had begun. Frontier justice, PNAC-style, was about to be unleashed, and America and the world would reap the whirlwind.

Chapter Four **The Politics of Personal Culpability and the Myth of the 180 Degree "Flip"**

"Fear not the Path of Truth, for the lack of People Walking on It."

—Robert Francis Kennedy

Looking back on how the Big Lie was sold to the American people, I find it ironic that I was cast by those doing the selling as one of the main "salesmen," so to speak. My high-profile resignation from the United Nations Special Commission in mid-August 1998, coupled with two televised appearances before Congressional committees in both the Senate and the House of Representatives, guaranteed that my message got widespread coverage. The only problem was, what got the coverage wasn't my message. Or, at least, not the entire message.

I resigned from UNSCOM in 1998 because I could no longer do my job as an inspector. From March 1996 until August 1998, inspections that I had planned and led in Iraq were prevented from carrying out their mission as tasked by the executive chairman on no fewer than twenty-five times. From November 1997 through August 1998, seven of these "stoppages" were the result of interference not by Saddam Hussein and the Iraqi regime, but rather direct intervention by Secretary of State Madeline Albright and–or the National Security Advisor Sandy Berger of the Clinton administration, who found the inspections politically unacceptable. In none of the cited instances did the Security Council, who mandated the inspections of UNSCOM and to whom we, as inspectors, reported, intervene in a meaningful way to maintain the integrity of the inspection process. Worse, because of the inaction of the Security Council, the Secretary General felt compelled to intervene, resulting in new inspection procedures that watered down the efficiency of the UNSCOM effort in Iraq.

The final straw came in the summer of 1998, when the United States pressured Richard Butler, the executive chairman of UNSCOM from 1997 until 1999, to shut down a sensitive intelligence operation I had been carrying out on behalf of UNSCOM inside Iraq since 1996, turning the capabilities inherent in this project (which included eavesdropping on the private conversations of Saddam Hussein and his inner circle of advisors) over to the United States without any UNSCOM input or control (or even access to the product derived from this effort), all the while continuing to operate under UNSCOM operational cover. In short, Richard Butler allowed the United States to use the unique access enjoyed by the UNSCOM inspectors through their Security Council mandate to spy on Saddam Hussein, totally corrupting the integrity of the overall operation.

In my letter of resignation, dated August 26, 1998, I set the tone of what I was all about by noting that I had, since 1991, "dedicated my professional life to the furtherance of the mandate of the Special Commission as set forth in relevant Security Council resolutions." Not secret U.S. policy objectives, not my own hidden personal agenda, but the mandate of a Chapter VII Security Council resolution that my own government sponsored and voted in support of. "As part of the Special Commission team," I wrote, "I have worked to achieve a simple end: the removal, destruction, or rendering harmless of Iraq's proscribed weapons. The sad truth is that Iraq today is not disarmed anywhere near the level required by Security Council resolutions." An accurate statement if there ever was one. Iraq cannot be considered disarmed until the weapons inspectors verify that the totality of Iraq's proscribed arsenal has been "removed, destroyed, or rendered harmless" in accordance with the will of the council. As of my resignation, this was not the case. This didn't mean that Iraq had weapons; it meant that those mandated with investigating the final disposition of these weapons couldn't verify the status of some 5 to 10 percent of the Iraqi arsenal, not an insignificant amount, especially if you are dealing with biological and chemical agent, where even minimal quantities can cause a great deal of grief.

UNSCOM's job was quantitative in nature, meaning that we had to account for everything. We were not permitted by the resolutions that mandated our work to apply qualitative analysis to the disarmament process. We knew that anthrax, especially anthrax produced in liquid bulk form (as was the totality of Iraq's stocks) had a shelf life of three years under ideal storage conditions, and that the last known batch was produced in 1991, and in any case, we blew up the factory in 1996. But this still didn't let Iraq off the hook for providing verifiable data which backed up their assertions that all biological weapons agent and associated material had been destroyed. One of the reasons we were so strict was that Iraq had lied to us about even having a biological weapons program in the first place, not acknowledging this capability until April 1995. We also knew that the chemical agent produced by Iraq between 1983 and 1988 (during the Iran–Iraq War) was of such a poor quality that it lost its viability after a few years, making our concerns over some 6,500 unaccounted-for munitions purely academic in nature. But Iraq was being uncooperative about other aspects of our chemical weapons investigation, especially on matters pertaining to VX nerve agent (something that, like their biological weapons program, Iraq had failed to declare to UNSCOM until 1995). For these and other reasons, I highlighted the incomplete status of our investigation by noting in my letter, "As you know, UNSCOM has good reason to believe that there are significant numbers of proscribed weapons and related components and the means to manufacture such weapons unaccounted for in Iraq today." An accurate statement.

As one of the lead investigators into the issue of Iraq's disarmament status, and the one responsible for heading the investigation into Iraq's concealment of its weapons from the inspectors, I put a great deal of importance behind the procedures of inspection. The integrity of the investigation process was extremely important. We had stringent requirements on not only what was required from Iraq, but also what we could and couldn't do. In holding Iraq accountable to the rule of law, we ourselves had to make sure we operated within the framework of the law as set forth by the Security Council in its resolutions. When we showed up at a facility in Iraq that had been designated for inspection, Iraq had an obligation to facilitate our immediate, unrestricted access to the site. We, in turn, had an obligation to stick to our disarmament mandate, all the while respecting the dignity, sovereignty, and legitimate national security interests of Iraq, regardless of what we might think personally about the odious nature of the regime.

It was a simple deal: We show up to inspect, you let us in, no questions asked, and we stick to our job of disarmament. But for this to work, Iraq had to let us in, and this was proving to be an issue. This is why I lamented the actions of the council in my letter of resignation, noting that "the recent decisions by the Security Council to downplay the significance of the recent Iraqi decision to cease cooperation with Commission inspectors clearly indicates that the organization which created the Special Commission in its resolution 687 (1991) is no longer willing and–or capable of the implementation of its own law, in this case an enforceable resolution passed under Chapter VII of the United Nations Charter. This abrogation of its most basic of responsibilities has made the Security Council a witting partner to an overall Iraqi strategy of weakening the Special Commission." If Iraq wouldn't let inspectors inspect, then we couldn't do our job as tasked by the executive chairman. If the Council refused to back us up in the face of this Iraqi obstruction, then we would never be able to do our job. To try and operate in such an environment would be, as I noted, an illusion. "The illusion of arms control," I wrote, "is more dangerous than no arms control at all."

We weren't in a position to give Iraq the benefit of the doubt, because, as I wrote in my letter, "Iraq has lied to the Special Commission and the world since day one concerning the true scope and nature of its proscribed programs and weapons systems. This lie has been perpetuated over the years through systematic acts of concealment." The only way to do our job effectively was for us, as inspectors, to have unimpeded, unrestricted access to sites we designated for inspection. "Inspections do work," I emphasized in my letter, "too well, in fact, prompting Iraq to shut them down all together . . . the issue of immediate, unrestricted access is, in my opinion, the cornerstone of any viable inspection regime, and as such is an issue worth fighting for. Unfortunately, others do not share this opinion, including the Security Council and the United States." I resigned in defense of the inspection process, without which there could be no inspections. Without inspections, there could be no disarmament. Without disarmament, Iraq would continue to constitute a clear and present risk to international peace and security, since it was the threat of Iraq's weapons of mass destruction programs that prompted the Security Council to mandate inspections in the first place.

On September 3, 1998, I found myself seated before a joint hearing of the Senate Foreign Relations and Armed

Services Committees, testifying about Iraq. I again stuck to my main theme: retaining the integrity of the inspection effort. "Iraq today is not disarmed," I said, "and remains an ugly threat to its neighbors and to world peace." I continued:

> Those American who think that this is important and that something should be done about it have to be deeply disappointed in our leadership. I'm here today to provide you with specific details about the scope and nature of interference by this administration in UNSCOM, the debilitating effect that such interference has on the ability of UNSCOM to carry out its disarmament mission in Iraq, and to appeal to the administration and to the Senate to work together to change America's Iraq policy back to what has been stated in the past: full compliance with the provisions of Security Council resolutions, to include enabling UNSCOM to carry out its mission of disarmament in an unrestricted, unhindered fashion. Only through the reestablishment of such a policy, clearly stated and resolutely acted upon, does the United States have a chance of resuming its leadership role in overseeing the effective and verifiable disarmament of Iraq so that neither we nor Iraq's neighbors in the Middle East will be threatened by Saddam Hussein's nuclear, chemical, or biological weapons or long-range ballistic missiles capable of delivering such weapons.

My appearance before the Senate was in the capacity of an investigator who had been thwarted in the conduct of his investigation. I was very careful in my language, underscoring the critical importance of my work—and the work of all other inspectors—while all the while emphasizing that this was about process. I didn't have a "smoking gun" of continued Iraqi possession of weapons of mass destruction, but rather a proven record of obstruction of our work, which caused concern about the underlying reasons behind this obstruction, and a stack of credible intelligence leads that needed to be thoroughly investigated, especially in light of the Iraqi obstruction. "We have clear evidence," I noted, "that Iraq is retaining prohibited weapons capabilities in the fields of chemical, biological, and ballistic-missile delivery systems of a range of greater than one hundred and fifty kilometers. And if Iraq has undertaken a concerted effort run at the highest levels inside Iraq to retain these capabilities, then I see no reason why they would not exercise the same sort of concealment efforts for their nuclear programs."

Senators Richard Lugar (R–Indiana) and Joe Biden (D–Delaware), the two senior members of the Senate Foreign Relations Committee, both spoke up in defense of a policy of containment, so to speak, even if it meant constraining weapons inspections. This point of view was articulated by Senator Lugar in a question to me, where he noted that "essentially we are in a situation, whether we've described it or articulated it to the public or not, that we're hopeful of keeping a Security Council majority, and certainly the big five, to keep a regime of sanctions on Iraq so that Iraq would not obtain the income really for truly explosive or dynamic developments. In our own way, although we've not articulated this, we've been willing to leave things at a dull roar in terms of whatever is going on in the hopes of staving off, through international cooperation, something that would be more explosive. Is that a reasonable policy?"

I couldn't disagree more. "The Special Commission has been handed," I replied, "what indeed is a good task—to rid the world of Iraqi weapons of mass destruction. And the Security Council, in passing its resolution under Chapter VII, said that is was an enforceable task." I continued:

> The Special Commission has worked closely with member states of the United Nations, to include the United States, on defining methodologies and tactics and inspection approaches toward disarming Iraq. And as recently as May 1997, the United States embraced our—the Special Commission's—concepts on how to approach the concealment effort. That's what makes this so frustrating, because this cooperation, this coordination was clearly reflected in the 6 April report by the president of the United States to Congress . . . that was the stated policy of the United States. However, following the president's report, by mid-April the red light had been given the Special Commission by the United States saying that we will not condone inspections of discovery—meaning the kind of inspections that I was charged with executing in Iraq—which would lead to confrontation. We would not support confrontation with Iraq over the right of inspections for the purpose of gaining access to sites . . . we are an inspection organization. We need to conduct inspections to find these weapons, and if you stop us from doing our job, what does that say? Iraq is allowed to have these weapons?

Senator Lugar tried to trap me into a discussion of American policy prerogatives. "If that has in fact been the administration's hope," he said, "to avoid confrontation and to keep the Security Council going—confrontation means military action. It means coming up against once again the hard issues that senators have talked about today . . . I would say that if that is what you are saying, however, you are, as—Senator Biden once again has pointed to the fact that hard issues are here; that is, to what extent is the American public, through its armed forces, through its representatives, prepared really to be credible?" I didn't bite, instead accurately noting that "the weapons inspection teams, to include the one that I was in charge of—we don't base our decisions to do inspections upon the internal domestic policies of any member state of the United Nations. Our job is clearly set forth in Security Council resolutions—to disarm Iraq through the process of inspection."

Next to take a swing at me was Senator Carl Levin (D–Michigan).

SEN. LEVIN: Yeah, but would you agree that it's important that if there's a threat of force, that that force be implemented and not just made and then ignored? If you're going to make a threat of force to enforce a policy, you darn well better carry out that threat if you are thwarted. Would you agree with that?

RITTER: Yes, sir. This is part of the cycle of confrontation and concession that I have been talking about, and we can't give concessions. If we have confrontation, it must have a resolution.

SEN. LEVIN: Yeah. Okay, and that means then if your threat of force is credible, it's got to be implementable, and there's got to be a will to use force if necessary once that threat is made. Now that's where we are. That's where we were when the Senate was looking at a resolution to see if we could support the use of force to implement that kind of a threat. But it's better not to make a threat if you're not going to carry it out than it is to make a threat and ignore it, 'cause you're really worse off if you make a threat and then not follow through with that threat. Would you agree with that?

RITTER: Senator, the threat was made back in April 1991.

SEN. LEVIN: No, I mean threat of force.

RITTER: The threat of force was made back in April 1991 when the Security Council together with the vote and pushing and backing of the United States passed the original cease-fire resolution. I don't see anything that would have caused the law to be altered. Iraq has not been disarmed. I would assume that that threat of force still exists today.

SEN. LEVIN: Would you agree though that it needs to be—it has to be credible if you're going to succeed?

RITTER: Yes, sir.

The hearing was going in a direction I didn't want. I wasn't here to lay down a case for war, but rather to insist that the United States support the integrity of the inspection process. Clearly, other Senators were operating under a different agenda. One of these was Senator Biden.

SEN. BIDEN: Thank you, Mr. Chairman. I envy your position. I sincerely do. I envy the ability to have such clarity on this issue. Let me ask you a question, do you think you should be the one to be able to decide when to pull the trigger?

RITTER: No, sir.

SEN. BIDEN: Isn't that what this is about? If you adopt the position that any time you are denied, your—and there's four groups out there, of inspectors—your—the group you headed—anytime you were denied, that that ipso facto requires the United States and the Security Council to act on what they said they would do, which is to use whatever means necessary to take on Saddam Hussein so you can get into that particular facility. Is that not correct? Is that not your position?

RITTER: Mr. Senator, I have a job to do—or I had a job to do, and that was to disarm Iraq in accordance with the provisions of—

SEN. BIDEN: No, I got that.

RITTER: —Security Council resolutions.

SEN. BIDEN: With all due respect, if you—I am not trying to be confrontational.

RITTER: Okay.

SEN. BIDEN: I am trying to get this as clear as I can. I really mean this now. You have an absolute logic; you put together a very tight syllogism here. You have indicated that your job is to disarm. The only way you can disarm is to have access. And the only way you can have access is either with permission on the part of Iraq, or if denied, forced access. Right?

RITTER: Compelled access, yes.

SEN. BIDEN: "Compelled." Well, okay, compelled. You sound like the lawyer, and I sound like the military guy. (Chuckles.) I mean, you know, compelled where I come from—when my old man said, "You're compelled," it meant "I was forced." I mean, it was a real simple proposition. It wasn't—you know, there wasn't much to debate. Now there is a clear logic to that, and that's what I mean when I say I respect your position. But that means that whenever you choose a target, that warrants inspection and you are denied, that ipso facto at that moment the only way your position can be satisfied or sustained is if the U.N. Security Council, or the United States acting unilaterally, uses force to guarantee access. Is not that true?

RITTER: Yes, sir.

SEN. BIDEN: Now that means that you get to choose the time and place when we would use force if we use force.

RITTER: No, sir.

SEN. BIDEN: Of course, you do. If you choose the site and it's denied—

RITTER: And we coordinate with the member states, to include the United States—

SEN. BIDEN: Exactly.

RITTER: —and prior to us going in, we have their agreement that this indeed is an inspection worth doing.

SEN. BIDEN: Okay. Inspection worth doing; everybody is agreed it's worth doing, and it gets stopped?

RITTER: Yes, sir.

SEN. BIDEN: At that moment, we're on automatic pilot as far as you're concerned—period. No ifs, ands or buts. Now I respect that. But now it seems to me the secretary of state might have a slightly different problem. The secretary of state might be sitting there and saying: "Now look over there on that side now. I remember so-and-so and so-and-so and so-and-so, and the twelve people on this side, they're all the ones that said they didn't want to use force. Now I am going to have to go tell the president now that we should—or Secretary Cohen—unleash whatever it takes to get it done." And our military assessment is the same as the major's. The major's assessment is, privately held but publicly acknowledged later, that air strikes alone aren't going to do this. Saddam's not going to cave on this. So, now, here's the deal. I recommended the president have at it, and let the chips fall where they may. A reasonable position for the secretary of defense and the secretary of state to take. But I respectfully suggest, major, I respectfully suggest they have responsibilities slightly above your pay grade—slightly above your pay grade—to decide whether or not to take the nation to war alone or to take the nation to war part-way, or to take the nation to war half-way. That's a real tough decision. That's why they get paid the big bucks. That's why they get the limos and you don't. I mean this sincerely. I'm not trying to be flip, because I think—and that's what I said at the outset. The reason why I'm glad you did what you did, we should come to our milk. We should make a decision. But in terms of whether the secretary of state has no more to consider than you do as the arms inspector—you didn't get in, didn't get my job done, get me in! Period. You made the deal, right? That's the deal. A deal's a deal. Get me in! Scott Ritter, I'm ready to go. That's not how it works.

Now, maybe it should work that way. But wouldn't you acknowledge that if you were president of the United States or the secretary of state you'd sit there and say, "Now, okay. Old Scottie boy didn't get in. We said he should get it. We want him to get in. It's important that he does get in. They're not going to let him in. So what are we going to do now? We know that France and Russia aren't going to be with us. We're quite confident China's not. We've already run those traps; they're not there. We're not sure whether the United States Senate is. But have at it, boys. Go get 'em. And by the way, Scott and the boys say air power's not enough." I think it's a legitimate debate, major. I think it's a legitimate debate. But I don't think we should be putting it in the context of, you have somebody up there at State saying "Now, look, how can we weasel out of this agreement? We don't want to let this guy

out there hanging. We're not this—" It's a very practical political decision. The same kind of decision General Powell
made. The same kind of decision President Bush made. Every
president and every secretary of state needs to do it. Like I
said, they get paid more than you, their job's a hell of a lot
more complicated than yours. They may have made the
wrong decision. And you brought it to light. We should
address it. We should say straight up where we are. And we
should do it. And for that, I thank you. But it's above your pay
grade. I yield the floor.

I fought back later in my testimony noting, that I wasn't there
to lobby for or against war. "What I'm doing," I said, "is holding a mirror up to the Senate, to this administration, and to the
American people, and I'm asking you to look into it. In 1991,
you tasked the Special Commission to carry out disarmament
inspections of Iraq. And you said that Iraq, if they don't do it,
because we passed this resolution under Chapter VII, we will
enforce this resolution. And in 1998, today, I stand before you
to say that, A, Iraq is not disarmed; and B, the United States,
as a member of the Security Council which gave us this mission, is doing other than it has said it wanted to do. It set forth
the policy on 6 April, and during the course of this summer,
on at least the two occasions that I'm directly familiar with, it
acted in a way that was in total contravention of that policy.
It said in April, 'Do teh inspections. We support you,' and in
July and in August, it said, 'Don't do the inspections.'"

But Biden's outburst got the media attention. In some
ways, Joe Biden's arrogance was the worst thing that happened to me and the cause I was supporting, not so much in

terms of putting me in my place (I stood my ground without flinching, and many Senators spoke up later in my defense), but rather putting me in a position of being someone under attack from one of Bill Clinton's most ardent supporters. Suddenly I was the darling of the neoconservative "get Clinton, get Iraq" crowd. I was fighting in defense of the integrity of the inspection regime. But now the debate was about the need to confront Saddam, a question of national will to wage war in defense of our security. William Kristol's *The Weekly Standard* sang my praises, as did archconservatives from George Will to Frank Gaffney. I was the poster child for the PNAC posse. In his own appearance before Congress, none other than Paul Wolfowitz rallied to my "cause," calling me "a public servant of exceptional integrity and moral courage, one of those individuals who is not afraid to speak the truth . . . now he is speaking the truth about the failures of the U.N. inspection regime in Iraq, even though those truths are embarrassing to senior officials in the Clinton administration. And the pressures he is being subjected to are far worse. After first trying to smear his character with anonymous leaks, the administration then took to charging that Mr. Ritter doesn't "have a clue" about U.S. policy toward Iraq and saying that his criticisms were playing into Saddam Hussein's hands by impugning UNSCOM's independence."[6]

My words were being twisted out of context, and used to support issues that had nothing to do with inspections. In October, 1998, during the debate over the soon to be passed Iraq Liberation Act, Senator Jesse Helms (R–North Carolina) underscored this in his statement to the Senate. "Mr.

President," he said, "I am an original co-sponsor of . . . the Iraq Liberation Act, for one simple reason: Saddam Hussein is a threat to the United States and a threat to our friends in the Middle East. This lunatic is bent on building an arsenal of weapons of mass destruction with a demonstrable willingness to use them. For nearly eight years the United States has stood by and allowed the U.N. weapons inspections process to proceed in defanging Saddam. That process is now in the final stages of collapse, warning that the U.S. cannot stand idly by hoping against hope that everything will work itself out. We have been told by Scott Ritter and others that Saddam can reconstitute his weapons of mass destruction within months." What I actually said was something quite different. It came in an exchange with Senator Sam Brownback (R–Kansas).

> SEN. BROWNBACK: In your opinion, *in the absence of a robust inspection regime* [emphasis added], how quickly could Iraq restart its weapons of mass destruction program?

> MR. RITTER: Iraq has—in my opinion, within a period of six months, simply put. Six months.

> SEN. BROWNBACK: Do you have any information as to whether they are continuing with it to even today?

> MR. RITTER: Yes, sir.

> SEN. BROWNBACK: You do?

> MR. RITTER: Yes, sir.

SEN. BROWNBACK: What's your opinion about that continuation of their weapons of mass destruction program today?

MR. RITTER: They're—Iraq has positioned itself today that *once effective inspection regimes have been terminated* [emphasis added], Iraq will be able to reconstitute the entirety of its former nuclear, chemical, and ballistic missile delivery system capabilities within a period of six months.

My emphasis was on inspections, and the need for inspections—robust inspections, as intended by the Security Council when it created UNSCOM. While war may be what was needed to enforce a Chapter VII resolution, I was not advocating one. But those who did were now using my "message" to support their cause, and the two, in the minds of many Americans, became inextricably entwined.

I never shied away from the fact that Iraq had not shown itself to be in compliance with its obligation to disarm. But I likewise never shied away from the need to maintain the legitimacy of the inspection effort, or else enforcement under Chapter VII of the U.N. Charter would be meaningless. Integrity was everything, as I pointed out to Senator Max Cleland (D–Georgia) during my Senate hearing. "I'd like to ask you," the decorated Vietnam War veteran said, "should we have taken out Saddam Hussein in 1991?" I responded forcefully and to the point. "Sir, I am here to speak based upon my experience as a weapons inspector, and with all due respect I would tarnish the objectivity of the Special Commission if I answered that question."

Integrity of the mandate was key, if we were to hold Iraq

accountable for its noncompliance, something I underscored in an exchange with Senator Paul Coverdell (R–Georgia).

SEN. COVERDELL: In an interview on CNN two days ago, on September 1st, Secretary of State Albright made the following statement: "There have been great inspections that have taken place in the last several years where we have made it possible for them [UNSCOM] to go to the Ministry of Defense, for them to go into a number of areas that had never been inspected before." Mr. Ritter, did you or anyone else at UNSCOM ever argue that there was compelling evidence to inspect the Iraqi Ministry of Defense for arms control reasons?

MR. RITTER: No, sir.

SEN. COVERDELL: But the secretary of state is clearly claiming that the United States "made it possible," quote unquote, for UNSCOM to inspect the Ministry of Defense. That would imply that UNSCOM wanted to conduct that inspection. Whose idea was it to conduct that inspection, UNSCOM's or the United States'?

MR. RITTER: The United States has been pressing the Special Commission to inspect the Ministry of Defense now for— since 1991, and both of the executive chairmans have repeatedly held off from authorizing this because there was no compelling arms control reason presented to them for the conduct of such inspection. In March, the Special Commission was again—or, in February, the Commission was confronted with a request—even a demand—by the

United States that the Ministry of Defense be included in the list of disarmament targets. And the executive chairman was confronted by members of his staff, to include myself, and reminded that we had no compelling arms control reason to do this, and that this was probably *heading down a slippery slope of confrontation which could not be backed up by our mandate.* [emphasis added]

"Iraq's disarmament obligations," I wrote in December 1998 in an oft-quoted article in *The New Republic*, "are set forth in a Chapter VII Security Council resolution, which mandates Iraq's compliance and authorizes the use of military force to compel it." I continued.

UNSCOM is the organization designated for overseeing Iraq's disarmament and verifying Iraq's long-term compliance. Thus, UNSCOM alone holds the key to unlocking the Iraqi disarmament issue. There is no endgame without UNSCOM . . . the world should demand a robust inspection regime and total Iraqi compliance. If Iraq refuses to do this, or if it is unduly obstructive, then the United States and the Security Council should seek to compel Iraq, through military force if necessary. Military strikes carried out for the purpose of enabling a vigorous UNSCOM to carry out its mandate are wholly justifiable.[7]

The other half of the equation I was articulating was that "Military strikes carried out for unilateral policy objectives not sustained by Security Council mandate are not justified." Unfortunately, that was the direction in which the Clinton administration headed. Under pressure from Congress in the aftermath of the passage of the Iraq Liberation Act, Bill Clinton needed to be seen as being decisive. The return of weapons inspectors to Iraq in November 1998, following lengthy diplomacy which only made the Clinton administration look even weaker, opened the door for a military showdown.

Iraq had been resisting the work of the UNSCOM inspectors since August 1998, when they ceased cooperating with American members of the inspection team, saying that these members were nothing more than CIA spies operating on behalf of the United States, not the Security Council. This decision by the Iraqis led to rampant speculation, led by the PNAC posse, as to what mischief Saddam Hussein and his scientists might be up to in the absence of the "serious" American inspectors, and rumors flew about stockpiles of deadly chemical and biological agents, a resurrected nuclear weapons programs, and secret missile factories. This hyping of the Iraqi threat, combined with the political realities surrounding the need, as cited by the Pentagon, to stop once and for all the "yo-yo" effect the repeated ramp up and ramp down to crisis the ongoing inspection drama prompted (at great expense to the U.S. taxpayer and to military readiness), led the president to conclude that the situation must be brought to a head, the inspection program terminated, and Saddam effectively contained by sanctions and aerial patrols over the no-fly zones. To implement this new Iraq strategy, the United States created a crisis that generated a myth used by those encouraging decisive confrontation with Iraq over the issue of weapons inspectors—that Saddam Hussein expelled the inspectors from Iraq, forcing President Clinton to attack. This myth was useful since it reinforced the logical construct that Saddam wanted the inspectors removed so he could reconstitute his lethal arsenal without the inconvenience of the prying eyes of international monitors. However, like all myths, this one isn't true. It wasn't Saddam Hussein or the Iraqi Government who gave weapons inspectors from the United Nations Special Commission (UNSCOM) the boot in 1998, but rather the United States. The United States ordered the inspectors removed from Iraq on the eve of Operation Desert Fox, a unilateral seventy-two-hour aerial bombardment of Iraq conducted without the approval of, or even in consultation with, the Security Council of the United Nations, which in theory at least was the organization with cognizance over the work of UNSCOM.

When confronted by the uncomfortable fact, those who supported Desert Fox continued to expand on the myth. The United States, so the argument went, was justified in ordering the UNSCOM inspectors removed for their own safety. Repeated Iraqi obstruction of the work of the inspectors, up to and including the critical denial of access to an UNSCOM inspection team trying to gain entry to an arms cache in downtown Baghdad, made the continued work of the inspectors impossible. Iraq's repeated flouting of its disarmament obligation, and its demonstrated unwillingness to part with its prohibited weapons, made it a menace to international peace and security that could no longer be ignored. The United States had no choice but to bomb Iraq, destroying the very arms factories Saddam was trying to preserve.

Unfortunately for those who embrace this myth, it simply doesn't hold water. The crisis of December 1998 actually had its roots in an earlier crisis, this one in the Summer of 1996, where UNSCOM inspectors (I was the deputy of this team) were stopped outside several military barracks associated with the security of Saddam Hussein. Rolf Ekeus, the distinguished Swedish diplomat who headed UNSCOM from 1991 to 1997, flew into Baghdad to resolve the stand-off. The solution came in the form of the so-called Modalities for the Inspection of Sensitive Sites, which required Iraq to provide immediate access to any site designated for inspection, with the proviso that the inspection team would be limited in size to four inspectors (unless something of a proscribed nature was discovered, in which case the site was fair game for as many inspectors as deemed required).

The sensitive site modalities held for over a year, until early October, 1997. Rolf Ekeus had left UNSCOM in June 1997, replaced by the Australian Richard Butler. Butler had taken an immediate dislike to the concept of sensitive site modalities, encouraged in no small part by his deputy, Charles Duelfer, a senior State Department official on asssignment to UNSCOM. The United States had opposed the concept of inspection modalities, and had been looking for an excuse to get rid of them. On October 1, 1997, when the Iraqis stopped an inspection team that I was heading from entering an area it deemed as presidential, Richard Butler made a decision that further obstructions of this sort would not be tolerated. In close consultation with the United States, Butler moved to eliminate the sensitive site modalities. However, when the matter was raised with Tariq Aziz during consultations in December, 1997, the best Richard could do was to negotiate an increase in the number of inspectors allowed during the initial entry of a site, from four to whatever the chief inspector felt was necessary to do the job. These new modalities were tested in March, 1998, when I led an inspection team that gained access to some of the most sensitive sites in Iraq, including the Ministry of Defense (which was entered with a team of eighteen inspectors). Intervention by Kofi Annan secured inspector access to Presidential Sites in April 1998.

Fast forward to August, 1998. The Iraqi Government, displeased with what it described as the pro-American bias of Richard Butler, limited its cooperation with UNSCOM inspectors to those sites subjected to monitoring work. All other inspection activity was halted. Iraq justified its decision by stating that inspections were being used as a front for the collection of intelligence by the United States. On October 31, 1998, Iraq shut down all inspection activity inside Iraq, stating that their could be no further cooperation with UNSCOM until economic sanctions were lifted, UNSCOM brought under the full control of the Security Council, and Richard Butler was removed from his post.

On November 10, 1998, acting under instructions from the acting U.S. Ambassador to the United Nations, Richard Butler ordered UNSCOM inspectors to evacuate Iraq, prompting speculation of an imminent U.S. military strike. Butler's precipitous actions angered many in the Security Council, especially Russia and France, who felt the council should have been consulted before such an action was taken, especially in light of the fact that the removal of the inspectors opened the door for an American attack, something many in the council wished to avoid. In this instance, diplomacy prevailed, and UNSCOM was permitted to return to work in Iraq to carry out the full range of its inspection activities. However, behind the scenes loomed the ever-present threat of American military power should Iraq fail to comply.

According to U.S. Government officials, on November 30, 1998, Richard Butler met with Sandy Berger, the Clinton administration's national security advisor, during which time a strategy was mapped out for Iraq. Berger was under pressure from the Department of Defense to bring an end to the cycle of crisis regarding Iraq, which was straining U.S. military resources. The Pentagon had a window of opportunity to strike Iraq in mid-December 1998 made possible by the overlapping of military units on rotation in the Persian Gulf. The Pentagon warned that after mid-December, it would be reorganizing its military posture in the Persian Gulf to one that supported containment of Iraq. Berger had one last opportunity for decisive military action. Butler was instructed to organize inspection activity designed to provoke Iraq into breaking its agreement to fully cooperate with UNSCOM. Deliberately controversial inspection sites would be selected, using intelligence provided by the United States and Great Britain. But the most provocative act would be left to UNSCOM: without consulting the Security Council, and acting at the behest of the United States, Richard Butler declared that the sensitive site modalities were null and void.

The Iraqis were notified of the nullification of the sensitive site modalities on December 8, 1998, during a meeting with UNSCOM inspectors in Baghdad. The Iraqis expressed shock at this declaration. The next day, when UNSCOM inspectors attempted to gain entry into a Ba'ath Party Headquarters in downtown Baghdad, the Iraqis invited them in, as long as the sensitive site modalities applied. The inspectors refused, saying the modalities no longer were in effect. Iraq then denied the team access, and the inspectors were withdrawn from the site. On December 11, 1998, while inspectors were still working in Iraq, Sandy Berger again met with Richard Butler to discuss how to best frame Butler's report to the Security Council about Iraq's level of cooperation with the inspectors. Following this meeting, in which both Butler and Berger had decided that the Iraqi blockage of inspectors at the Ba'ath Party site was damning enough to justify a U.S. military strike (the fact that Iraq was, as the two men spoke, providing inspectors with immediate access to a series of sensitive security installations, was deemed irrelevant). In order to prevent an accumulation of further instances of Iraqi cooperation, Richard Butler, acting on the advise of Sandy Berger, ordered the inspection teams withdrawn from Iraq.

Sandy Berger reported the intended tone of the Butler report to President Clinton, who was at that time overseas, in Israel. Based upon this information, the president, on Sunday, December 13, 1998, gave the orders for a military strike against Iraq. On Monday, in keeping with the script, Richard Butler drafted his report to the Security Council about Iraq's cooperation with the work of UNSCOM. Butler was in continuous contact throughout the day with Sandy Berger and other U.S. Government officials about the language of the report, making several trips to the U.S. Mission for conversations on secure phones. Once the language had been fine tuned to U.S. specifications, Butler released the report to the Security Council members and the Secretary General. That evening, again under direct orders from the acting U.S. Ambassador to the United Nations, and in violation of the assurances he had given France and Russia that no such action would be made without consulting the Security Council, Richard Butler ordered all UNSCOM inspectors withdrawn from Iraq.

Alarmed by the report submitted by Richard Butler, the Security Council convened a session on December 16, 1998. While Richard Butler was making a formal presentation of his report to the council, the United States, together with Great Britain, initiated Operation Desert Fox. The bombing campaign was justified on the basis of Butler's report, even though the report had yet to be presented to the council for discussion. The main reason cited for the Desert Fox attacks, according to President Clinton, was to destroy Iraq's capability to produce chemical, biological, nuclear, and long-range ballistic missiles. Only a dozen or so sites bombed could be described as falling into this category. All were sites considered to be dual-use in nature, meaning that they had a stated purpose which was not illegal, but also possessed certain capabilities that could be used for prohibited purposes. For this reason, UNSCOM had since 1994 monitored activity at all of these sites (and hundreds more), making sure no proscribed activity took place. UNSCOM knew in December 1998 that these sites were doing nothing that could be described as being in contravention of Iraq's disarmament obligation, and yet they were bombed.

Most of the targets bombed during Operation Desert Fox had nothing to do with weapons manufacturing. Ninety seven "strategic" targets were struck during the seventy-two-hour campaign; eighty-six were solely related to the security of Saddam Hussein—palaces, military barracks, security installations, intelligence schools, and headquarters. Without exception, every one of these sites had been subjected to intrusive on-site inspection by UNSCOM inspectors (most of these inspections had been led by me), and their activities were well-known and certified as not being related to the mandate of UNSCOM. Iraq had protested UNSCOM's inspection of these sites citing national security concerns, but the modalities for sensitive site inspections applied, and inspectors gained access. The information gathered during these inspections was passed, as part of an ongoing cooperation between the CIA and UNSCOM, to the U.S. government, which then used the data to target their bombs. The purpose of Operation Desert Fox was clear to all familiar with these sites: Saddam Hussein, not Iraq's weapons of mass destruction, was the target.

In the aftermath of Operation Desert Fox, Iraq refused to allow UNSCOM inspectors to return, citing their close links with U.S. intelligence and the fact that the UNSCOM Chief, Richard Butler, was taking direct orders from the U.S. Government. President Clinton's actions in Desert Fox, carried out in unilateral fashion, accomplished what he had set out to do—destroy the inspection apparatus. This was exactly what I had warned about back in September during my Senate testimony, actions which sent America down a slippery slope of confrontation not backed up by Security Council mandate—illegal actions. This was not what I had resigned to accomplish, and I felt more than a little bit responsible for the direction things were headed. I felt I had no choice but to do my best to clear up the record, and see if there was a way to get the inspection issue back on track. I had the advantage of having access to the bully pulpit, given my high profile resignation. I had a book deal, and a television contract with NBC News. I decided to try and do the right thing—continue telling the truth.

Now came the hard part—trying to articulate a case for the restoration of the legitimacy of U.N.-mandated weapons inspections while opposing the rush to war being articulated by the PNAC posse. This wasn't going to be easy, as I found out while delivering a talk to the pro-Israeli "Washington Institute for Near-East Policy" on the occasion of the publication of my book *Endgame* in March, 1999. "The only way to guarantee a regime removal," I said, a clear reference to the newly-passed Iraq Liberation Act, "is through military force by the United States. A victory of opposition groups, however well trained, over Saddam's forces would be very unlikely. The opposition would succeed only if American ground troops were sent to Iraq in sufficient quantity—a move that would meet significant resistance from many Americans." There was a noticeable shifting of some of the audience members in their seats. This was not what they had expected to hear from me. I continued:

> Ongoing American threats to remove the Iraqi regime can hardly be expected to increase Saddam's willingness to comply with weapons inspectors. As long as Saddam feels threatened, he will try to retain his weapons of mass destruction capability . . . The United States should consider diplomatic engagement of Iraq. The engagement would require that

Saddam demonstrate he has abandoned pursuing weapons of mass destruction. Then, there could be a discussion that would center on the economic reconstruction of Iraq, aimed at generating regional stability. The United States could use more face-saving measures, such as finding a framework for the expansion of Iraqi oil sales or cooperating with European banks to underwrite loans to the Iraqis and to help facilitate a realistic repayment schedule . . .[8]

At this point Frank Gaffney, a member of the PNAC posse who had, just months earlier, been promoting me, albeit tongue in cheek, as a replacement for Madeline Albright as secretary of state,[9] leapt to his feet. "You have completely lost your mind!" he shouted, before stomping out of the room. Several others followed suit.

The PNAC posse was pushing for a war with Iraq, using such a war as a vehicle to promote their own vision of American global hegemony. I was pushing for the rule of law. The two were mutually exclusive. It was going to be a fight, one I was committed to because it was about truth and things not only that I believed in, but believed my country stood for, regardless of the so-called vision being peddled by the PNAC posse. But it was not going to be an easy fight. Having embraced me as their poster child, the PNAC posse now had to disassociate themselves from Scott Ritter, the heretic, as soon as possible. To do this, they would employ every trick in the muckrakers book. I would be vilified, demonized, belittled, and smeared, all in the name of "truth," which of course—the PNAC code word for the Big Lie. Within a month my publisher stopped promoting my book, and NBC

News would terminated my contract. The war in Kosovo was cited by both as the reason, but the underlying theme was clear: I had gotten "off message," and as such was no longer convenient to the corporate mentality of "don't rock the boat." Score one for the PNAC posse. But while the bully pulpit may have been lost, the results were temporary.

The fight was just beginning.

Chapter Five **Selling the Big Lie**
Saddam Hussein as Reality Television

"If the truth doesn't save us, what does that say about us?"

—Lois McMaster Bujold

And, just like that, the war was over.

Like many, I sat and watched the war unfold before me live on television, courtesy of the many embedded reporters. My stomach churned at the thought of the Iraqis unveiling their hidden stockpiles of chemical weapons, unleashing them in a toxic cloud on our troops. I didn't believe they existed, but given the forcefulness of the Bush administration's assertions to the contrary, I had gnawing doubts.

Even Colin Powell, the sole moderate in the Bush administration's national security team, who was also not a member of the PNAC posse, had proclaimed the existence of these weapons in his presentation to the Security Council on February 5, 2003. "There can be no doubt," Powell told us, "that Saddam Hussein has biological weapons and the capability to rapidly produce more, many more. And he has the ability to dispense these lethal poisons and diseases in ways that can cause massive death and destruction. If biological weapons seem too terrible to contemplate, chemical weapons are equally chilling."

And to prove his point, he played intercepted radio communications that seemed to reinforce his assertions.

"*Remove. Remove,*" the voices spoke to us.

"*The expression, the expression,*" came the reply. "*I got it.*"

"*Nerve agents. Nerve agents. Wherever it comes up.*"

I didn't think Iraq had such weapons. "Well, we know that they do," Colin Powell told the world. "And this kind of conversation confirms it. Our conservative estimate is that Iraq today has a stockpile of between 100 and 500 tons of chemical weapons agent. That is enough agent to fill 16,000 battlefield rockets."

Academic number crunching? No, said Powell. "Saddam Hussein has chemical weapons . . . and we have sources who tell us that he recently has authorized his field commanders to use them. He wouldn't be passing out the orders if he didn't have the weapons or the intent to use them . . . we know from sources that a missile brigade outside Baghdad was disbursing rocket launchers and warheads containing biological warfare agents to various locations, distributing them to various locations in western Iraq."

During the war we were repeatedly bombarded with reports about the mythical "Red Line" around Baghdad, where Saddam was concentrating his chemical and biological weapons. The munitions were being handed out to the Republican Guard, we were told. When we cross the "Red Line," our troops will be "slimed" by the enemy's deadly toxic arsenal. Almost no one paid attention to the caveat the U.S. military was putting on the "Red Line." Coalition forces were attacking the Iraqis relentlessly, trying to interdict and prevent any attempt by the Iraqis to use their chemical and biological weapons. "The rest of the story is known only to the regime, and we will not ever know that," Brigadier General Vincent Brooks, the U.S. Central Command spokesman said on April 3 from his headquarters in Qatar. "If we're successful, they will never be used, and this red line will have been something that we just conceived and it was not real. And that's fine."[10]

Just conceived. Not real. No, General, it is not fine. Not with me, not with the American people, not with the world. We were told that this threat was genuine, not conceptual. And yet that is all it turned out to be. A figment of someone's imagination. We now know that as early as September, 2002, at the moment Sheriff Bush was delivering his ultimatum to the Security Council about the threat posed by Iraqi weapons of mass destruction, including chemical weapons, when the PNAC posse was lying to everyone they could corner, including Congress, about this mythological threat of nation-killing significance, the Defense Intelligence Agency, which one would hope General Brooks was familiar with, was saying the complete opposite. "There is no reliable information on whether Iraq is producing or stockpiling chemical weapons, or whether Iraq has—or will—establish its chemical warfare agent production facilities." The report noted that Iraq's ability to produce chemical weapons was "constrained by its stockpile of key chemical precursors and by the destruction of all known CW (chemical weapons) production facilities during Operation Desert Storm and during subsequent UNSCOM inspections."[11] This report was submitted at the same time Tony Blair was releasing his now-disgraced "dossier" on Iraqi capabilities, which crowed about Iraq's ability to deploy chemical and biological munitions within forty-five minutes.

On May 30, 2003, another shockwave rocked Team Bush. Lieutenant General James Conway, the commander of the 1st Marine Expeditionary Force, said he had been convinced by the repeated assertions made by U.S. intelligence before and during the war that shells with chemical warheads had been distributed to Republican Guard units around Baghdad. "It was a surprise to me . . . that we have not uncovered weapons, as you say, in some of the forward dispersal sites," the blunt Marine commander said. "Believe me, it's not for lack of trying," he added. "We've been to virtually every ammunition supply point between the Kuwaiti border and Baghdad, but they're simply not there . . . we were simply wrong."[12]

The Bush administration justified its war with Iraq based on the threat posed to the United States by Iraqi weapons of mass destruction—chemical, biological, and nuclear weapons and long range ballistic missiles. Three months after the start of the war, with Iraq fully occupied by U.S.-led forces, no such weapons (or related production capability) had been found. This wasn't for a lack of trying. The United States had been preparing for this weapons hunt since November of 2002. At that time, a U.S. Army Field Artillery Brigade turned in its guns and was reconfigured as a weapons inspection unit known as the 75th Exploitation Task Force, or XTF. The 75th XTF toured Iraq for nearly two months, finding no weapons of mass destruction or related manufacturing capability despite a checklist of hundreds of sites provided by U.S. intelligence.

Condoleezza Rice, the Bush's national security advisor, has indicated that Iraq had assembled a "virtually inspection-proof" system for hiding its weapons programs, and that it will take some time for the United States to untangle the Iraqi web of deception. For this reason, the United States shipped out the 75th XTF, and replaced it with an Iraq Survey Group, to be headed by Army Major General Keith Dayton. However, the Iraq Survey Group will not be spending most of its time looking for the missing weapons. Instead, the new team will search for and exploit Iraqi documents to try and assemble a circumstantial case of Iraqi noncompliance.

If the repeated mis-identification of Iraqi "weapons sites" by U.S. investigators were not evidence enough, the deployment of the Iraq Survey Group should scream out for the need to return properly mandated U.N. weapons inspectors to resume the task of completing Iraq's disarmament. The United States lacks any credibility when it comes to the search for Iraqi weapons. The fact that the Bush administration desperately needs to find something to sustain its prewar allegations about the nature of the Iraqi threat is proof positive of the need for an objective, impartial investigatory body. U.N. weapons inspectors, operating under Security Council mandate, are the only option in this regard, and should return to Iraq as soon as possible. But this is vehemently opposed by

the Bush administration. This continued obstructionist attitude, combined with the continued failure on the part of the
U.S.-led coalition to find any weapons of mass destruction in
Iraq, only accelerates the collapse of trust and confidence
around the world in the administration of George W. Bush
and the United States as a whole. The fact that one of the chief
architects for this war, arch-PNAC posse member Paul
Wolfowitz, has admitted the whole thing was a set-up only
further complicates matters. "For bureaucratic reasons,"
Wolfowitz confessed to Vanity Fair in an interview published
in the May 28, 2003 issue, "we settled on one issue, weapons
of mass destruction [as justification for invading Iraq]
because it was the one reason everyone could agree on."

Not because it was the right thing to do.

Not because we had overwhelming evidence that Iraq had
these weapons.

Because this was the Big Lie Team Bush was selling.

Paul Wolfowitz's comments set off a wave of protest
around the world, nowhere more spectacularly so than in
Great Britain, where Bush's staunch ally Tony Blair found
himself in very hot water. The credibility of the United States
has come under attack in a major way around the world. This
lack of confidence in the integrity of the United States does-
n't portend well for the ongoing war on terror, which even
prior to the Iraq War debacle had hit a dangerous impasse.
The rapid military campaign in Afghanistan, which saw the
demise of the Taliban and the scattering of Osama bin
Laden's al Qaeda, has stalled. American troops, together with
the forces of their allies, have become mired in a counterin-
surgency campaign which finds them confronting the forces

of tribalism more often than the forces of terror. Concerns over the difficult situation inside Afghanistan have prevented the United States from supporting an expansion of the International Security Assistance Force (ISAF), guaranteeing that the stability promised to the people of Afghanistan following the American-led intervention will be limited to the capital city of Kabul and its immediate environs, if that. As a result, the unrest in Afghanistan is actually creating a situation in the countryside that is conducive for a return of the Taliban and al Qaeda. The Taliban is resurgent, re-occupying and controlling increasingly large swaths of territory inside Afghanistan. Al Qaeda is far from dead, recent terror attacks proving that it remains active in Afghanistan and around the world. Osama bin Laden and many of his senior staff are still on the loose, and actively involved in coordinating the actions of al Qaeda. Sheriff Bush and his PNAC posse have proclaimed victory in Afghanistan. If what we are witnessing in Afghanistan is victory, please don't show me defeat.

In a dramatic landing straight out of *Top Gun* on the aircraft carrier U.S.S. *Abraham Lincoln*, U.S. Air National Guard fighter pilot turned Vietnam War deserter turned (sort of) U.S. Naval Aviator George W. Bush proclaimed victory in Iraq. This "victory" has many parallels with the "victory" we achieved in Afghanistan.

Saddam (as of mid-June, 2003) has yet to be captured.

American troops are still fighting and dying in combat operations.

Massive areas of the countryside are outside the control of U.S. occupation forces.

Anti-American sentiment is on the rise.

Watching the American "victors" operate in Iraq is a lot like watching a victim who has fallen into a patch of quicksand—a lot of thrashing around that, with each exertion, sucks the poor individual ever deeper into the bog. The United States is waist deep in a quagmire called Iraq, and yet we continue to deny it. But no matter how many times we proclaim victory, the simple act of saying it does not make it so. And the fact that our government continues to lie about weapons of mass destruction only precludes the possibility of some nation or group of nations coming to our assistance and helping us to extricate ourselves from the mess we've made.

We really have no one to blame but ourselves. Yes, the Bush administration sold us the Big Lie concerning Iraqi weapons of mass destruction, but we collectively bought into it. The media, Congress, and the people of the United States—we are all collectively culpable. We didn't ask enough questions, we didn't demand enough answers, and when someone had the gall to do so, we played "see no evil, speak no evil, hear no evil" in an effort to avoid considering that, when it came to Iraq's weapons of mass destruction, the emperor had no clothes.

It is not as though the facts to counter the Bush administration's claims were not made available to the American public or the world. I had made it my personal crusade to make myself available to counter the Big Lie. The PNAC posse may have conspired to deny me access to the bully pulpit, but I refused to back down. I wrote opinion pieces for the *New York Times*, the *Washington Post*, and the *Boston Globe*, among others, which ripped into the contradictory policies of the Clinton administration toward Iraq. The problem, I noted in the *Times* on August 16, 1999, was that the United States "can't demand compliance with Security Council resolutions while simultaneously shunning the Security Council by pursuing a unilateral campaign to remove Saddam from power. Until the United States recognizes that its policy is inherently contradictory, we won't achieve either disarmament or Saddam Hussein's removal from power. Disarmament requires fashioning a consensus that is acceptable to all Security Council members; ousting Saddam entails the commitment of American combat power. Neither option is ideal, but neither stands a chance if they're attempted in tandem." I concluded by emphasizing what had become the centerpiece of my counter-policy (the one which so infuriated Frank Gaffney and the PNAC): "The United States should pursue a diplomatic solution to this problem. We should support the lifting of economic sanctions in exchange for the resumption of meaningful inspections. Such a course would take a step toward reuniting and reinvigorating the Security Council. It would also bring credibility to our foreign policy in ways . . . military intervention never can."

No one listened. The drums of war were already softly pounding, unheard by all except those beating them. The Big Lie had been unleashed on the American public, and no one was willing to listen to a rogue former inspector who had, according to the PNAC, done a complete one hundred and eighty degree flip in his own position.

I struggled to correct that impression. In June 2000, I published a lengthy article in *Arms Control Today* entitled "The Case for the Qualitative Disarmament of Iraq," In it I wrote:

As the situation stands today, Iraq and the Security Council are deadlocked. There is no hope for the return of inspectors to Iraq anytime soon. With each passing day, concern increases over the status of Iraq's WMD programs because there are no inspectors in place to monitor them. Unless the Security Council can come up with a compromise, the situation will only continue to deteriorate.

What is often overlooked in the debate over how to proceed with Iraq's disarmament is the fact that from 1994 to 1998 Iraq was subjected to a strenuous program of ongoing monitoring of industrial and research facilities that could be used to reconstitute proscribed activities. This monitoring provided weapons inspectors with detailed insight into the capabilities, both present and future, of Iraq's industrial infrastructure. It allowed UNSCOM to ascertain, with a high level of confidence, that Iraq was not rebuilding its prohibited weapons programs and that it lacked the means to do so without an infusion of advanced technology and a significant investment of time and money.

Given the comprehensive nature of the monitoring regime put in place by UNSCOM, which included a strict export-import control regime, it was possible as early as 1997 to determine that, from a qualitative standpoint, Iraq had been disarmed. Iraq no longer possessed any meaningful quantities of chemical or biological agent, if it possessed any at all, and the industrial means to produce these agents had either been eliminated or were subject to stringent monitoring. The same was true of Iraq's nuclear and ballistic missile capabilities. As long as monitoring inspections remained in place, Iraq presented a WMD-based threat to no one.

The success of the UNSCOM monitoring regime may hold the key to unlocking the current stalemate between Iraq and the Security Council. The absolute nature of the disarmament obligation set forth in Resolution 687 meant that anything less than 100 percent disarmament precluded a finding of compliance. There was no latitude for qualitative judgments. As such, the world found itself in a situation where the considerable accomplishments of the UNSCOM weapons inspectors—the elimination of entire categories of WMD and their means of production—were ignored in light of UNSCOM's inability to verify that every aspect of these programs was fully accounted for. Quantitative disarmament (the accounting of every last weapon, component, or bit of related material) took precedence over qualitative disarmament (the elimination of a meaningful, viable capability to produce or employ weapons of mass destruction).

If the Security Council redefines Iraq's disarmament obligation along more meaningful—and politically and technically viable—qualitative standards, UNMOVIC should be able to reconstitute UNSCOM's monitoring program and rapidly come to closure on all outstanding disarmament issues. If such a disarmament program is linked with the lifting of economic sanctions upon a finding of compliance, Iraq will almost certainly agree to cooperate.

I advanced my argument carefully, backing up my assertions with documents drawn from my experience as a weapons inspector. Prior to the publication of this article, I had tried to advance this approach with members of the Senate Foreign Relations Committee. Only Senator Charles Hagel

(R–Nebraska) had the courage to meet me face-to-face, and in a lengthy meeting acknowledged his great concern over what was transpiring. He admitted that the data on the Iraqi threat was weak, and that inspections represented the best way forward, but he cautioned me: "Don't expect any 'Profile in Courage' moments out of any member of Congress on the issue of Iraq," he said. "The political climate won't permit it." This was echoed by Joe Biden's staff. After first condemning me as a traitor who belonged in jail for speaking "out of school" about U.S. policy on Iraq, Biden's staff later agreed that the current policy was a failure. "But we will never go against the president in an election year," they said. Senator John Kerry (D), the Massachusetts war hero, did talk to me over the phone. "Write it all down, Scott," he said. "Send it to me. I'll read it." I did, in the *Arms Control Today* article, and I made sure that a copy was sent to Kerry, and all the senators. No one ever responded. Richard Butler, my former boss, got on national television and decried the concept of qualitative disarmament as being "fundamentally flawed."

September 11, 2001, came and went, and I watched with concern and consternation as the rookie president from Texas got lassoed into a war with Iraq by the PNAC posse. The smoke was still rising from the wreckage of the World Trade Center when Paul Wolfowitz briefed George W. Bush that terror could never be defeated until the head of the snake— Saddam Hussein—had been cut off. This was on September 12, 2001, one day after the attack. The PNAC posse took no time in crassly manipulating the death and suffering of that horrible event for their own political gain. They wanted regime removal in Iraq. They wanted a new strategy for dominating the world. As of September 10, 2001, it had been denied them. September 11, 2001, in their minds, changed everything. They had a cause, and now they had a rallying cry. "Let's Roll!" they cried, perverting the heroic words of an American who gave his life, together with others, trying to regain control of a hijacked airliner before the terrorists could crash it into another building. "Let's Roll!" Wrapping themselves in patriotic red, white, and blue, the PNAC posse were really wolves in sheeps' clothing, disguising from the American public that the real hijacking taking place was the national security of the United States, shanghaied by this cabal of neoconservative ideologues who were advancing their own warped vision of American global hegemony on the graves of so many innocent lives.

For some strange reason, I had been approached in October 2001 by Fox News, the mouthpiece of the PNAC, to be an on-air analyst regarding the war on terror and the Iraq crisis. It was a six-month deal, one that I'm sure Fox News regretted inking almost immediately. On every appearance, I took issue with the Bush administration's spinning of the war in Afghanistan and the crisis with Iraq. The frustration inside Fox was palpable. They were paying me money to appear on television, but instead of supporting me, they did their level best to contradict and embarrass me. Nearly every appearance on Fox News became an opportunity for one PNAC posse member or another to shout and sneer at me, questioning my patriotism and denouncing my opinions as "fantasy." I had just finished making a documentary film about UNSCOM and the disarming of Iraq entitled *In Shifting Sands*. It was a solid piece of documentary film making, and had done very well at the Hot Springs Documentary Film Festival in its premier airing in October 2001. Rather than embrace the film and show it to the public, News Corporation, the Rupert Murdoch media machine that owns Fox News, used another one of its outlets, the neoconservative opinion journal *The Weekly Standard* to run a front-page story on me as in the November 2001 issue calling me "Saddam's American Apologist."

The article was derived from a lengthy phone interview with Steven Hayes, a feature writer for the *Standard*. But Hayes was much less than honest in his depiction of that interview, or the accompanying research. He wanted to write a story about me, regardless of the truth. I took money from Saddam, he said, to make the film. Nothing was further from the truth: my production company received $400,000 from an American citizen named Shakir Alkahfaji, money which was derived from Shakir's own assets and which had no link whatsoever with the Iraqi government. I had never, and would never, take a red cent from the Iraqi government, something I had made perfectly clear to Mr. Hayes. But he chose to stick to his story line, not the facts. Fox News wanted me smeared, and Hayes was the character assassin hired to do the job. Later, when it became clear that I was prevailing in every appearance on Fox, my employers took a different tack. They had an exclusive contract with me, meaning that I could only appear on Fox News. So they simply stopped using me, effectively silencing my voice. The contract with Fox expired in April, 2002. Fox made no effort to renew the deal. I didn't shed any tears.

By the spring of 2002, war fever was already high here in America, and Sheriff Bush and his PNAC posse began working on exporting it abroad. A series of high-level officials, including Rumsfeld and Wolfowitz, had paraded before NATO, trying to get that organization to embrace and support a war with Iraq, citing the threat posed to the transatlantic organization by Iraq's weapons of mass destruction. With the arrogance typical of the PNAC, the American officials refused to take any questions concerning the specific nature of the threats cited. I was scheduled to travel to France for meetings with French government officials and antiwar activists, and certain delegations in NATO, hearing of my pending arrival in Europe, asked if I could appear before a NATO committee to give testimony on Iraq. The Bush administration, hearing of this, vetoed the idea. Instead, I was invited to speak during a formal luncheon hosted by the Luxembourg ambassador. The American delegation boycotted the event, but the British did send a delegation. I fielded all questions concerning Iraq, and so embarrassed the British representative, who had attempted to ambush me with a prepared list of questions, that he tossed aside the document after getting less than half-way through. Following my presentation, many of the NATO delegations wrote letters to the United States, demanding more answers and questioning the veracity of the American briefings they had heard to date. According to an eyewitness, the U.S. ambassador to NATO, John Burns, was so enraged over my presentation, that he condemned the Luxembourg ambassador for hosting an event that gave the podium to a "known enemy of the state."

If I could succeed in getting NATO to seriously question the Bush administration's stance on Iraq through one briefing, I thought, imagine what might happen if I could orchestrate a repeat of the September 1998 Senate hearings? I tried calling the Senators directly to see if they would consider such a hearing. None took my call directly. John Kerry's staff lamely stated that "the time was not right" for such hearings. I wouldn't accept that answer. Throughout the summer of 2002 I actively pushed the idea of public hearings in Congress to debate the issue of war with Iraq and the threat posed by Iraqi weapons of mass destruction. I initiated a campaign of op-ed article writing, taking on the PNAC posse in newspapers from Boston to Los Angeles. With the assistance of the Traprock Peace Center, an antiwar activist group based in Massachusetts, I traveled to the home states of key senators in the Foreign Relations Committee, conducting town hall-style forums and meeting with the editorial staffs of newspapers. In Kansas, Massachusetts, Indiana, and Maryland major newspapers ran editorials calling for more specificity about the Iraqi threat. All I asked when I met with the editorial boards was for specific proof of an Iraqi threat before we went to war. The editorial boards agreed. And the pressure started to mount. By July, the senators could no longer ignore the growing demands for a hearing, and the Senate Foreign Relations Committee buckled, announcing two days of hearings on the nature of the Iraqi threat and the proper direction for America's Iraq policy.

"Without prejudging any particular course of action—including the possibility of staying with nonmilitary options—we hope to start a national discussion of some critical questions," the two senior members of the Senate Foreign Relations Committee wrote in an opinion piece published in the *New York Times* on July 31, 2002, the day the hearings began. Then they went and pre-ordained the outcome of their sham trial. "First, what threat does Iraq pose to our security? How immediate is the danger? President Bush is right to be concerned about Saddam Hussein's relentless pursuit of weapons of mass destruction. It's true that other regimes hostile to the United States and our allies have, or seek to acquire, chemical, biological, and nuclear weapons. What makes Mr. Hussein unique is that he has actually used them—against his own people and against his Iranian neighbors. And for nearly four years, Iraq has blocked the return of United Nations weapons inspectors. We need to explore Mr. Hussein's track record in acquiring, making, and using weapons of mass destruction and the likelihood he would share them with terrorists. We also need a clear assessment of his current capabilities, including conventional forces and weapons." The senators precluded from consideration any discussion that might contradict their preconceived notions that Iraq had weapons of mass destruction and related programs that posed a threat to the United States. They stacked the witness list. Despite thousands of letters, phone calls and emails demanding that I and other critics of the administration's policies be allowed to give testimony, Biden and Lugar only invited those who they knew could deliver on the scripted outcome—regime removal. The PNAC posse now had control of the legislative process, as well.

"It would be a tragedy if we removed a tyrant in Iraq, only to leave chaos in his wake. The long-suffering Iraqi people need to know a regime change would benefit them. So do Iraq's neighbors," said Senator Joseph Biden, chairman of the U.S. Senate Committee on Foreign Relations in his opening statement. The kangaroo court he presided over was to convene for two days. On July 31, so-called independent experts shared their views on the nature of the threat posed by the current Iraqi regime and possible responses. The August 1 panel of speakers focused on examining the breadth of U.S. obligations after the regime of Saddam Hussein is no longer in power. There was to be no discussion on the merits of a regime removal policy. "We need a better understanding of what it would take to secure Iraq and rebuild it economically and politically," Biden said.

Talk about prejudging the outcome of the discussion.

"It may be too late to stop productions of weapons," Khidir Hamza, director of the Council on Middle Eastern Affairs and one of the first of the "independent" witnesses to testify, told the Senate Foreign Relations Committee. "Even if weapons inspectors go in, there is very little human intelligence that will help them," he said. In short, the inspectors will never find Iraq's nuclear weapons, which may be hidden underground. "With little or no human intelligence it is difficult to see how anything short of regime change will help," said Hamza, the man whom Hussein Kamal, Saddam's son-in-law, called a "big liar." Nothing short of getting rid of Saddam would stop the weapons developments and impending threats they pose, the computer programmer turned self-proclaimed "bomb maker" for Saddam said. The timing of Hamza's testimony conveniently coincided with statements made by Defense Secretary Donald Rumsfeld one day prior, in which Rumsfeld told reporters that Iraq is providing safe harbor to al Qaeda terrorists and is working on building biological, chemical and nuclear weapons that Iraqi leader Saddam Hussein would be willing to share with the terror network. "They have chemical weapons and biological weapons and they have an appetite for nuclear weapons and have been working on them for a good many years, and there's an awful lot we don't know about their programs," Rumsfeld said, adding that even if inspectors returned, Iraq would be unlikely to allow the kinds of inspections needed to uncover all its weapons projects. "It would take such a thoroughly intrusive inspection regime agreed to and then lived up to by Iraq that it's difficult to comprehend—even begin to think—that they might accept such a regime," Rumsfeld said. "It would have to be without notice. It would have to be any-where, anytime."

Nobody ever said the PNAC posse couldn't choreograph a song and dance show, especially when so ably assisted by their new-found allies in the Senate. Khidir Hamza—the so-called expert witness—was followed on the witness stand by Richard Butler, the former Executive Chairman of UNSCOM known for his willful embrace of PNAC policies and his rejection of the truth. "It is essential to recognize that the claim made by Saddam's representatives, that Iraq has no weapons of mass destruction, is false. Everyone concerned, from Iraq's neighbors, to the U.N. Security Council and Secretary General of the U.N., is being lied to," Butler said, himself lying. Despite years of attempted international weapons inspection, Butler said, Iraq still has an array of biological weapons and missiles tipped with anthrax. He offered no compelling evidence to sustain this allegation. Like Hamza, he simply spoke, and the Senate recorded. "We do not know and never have known fully the quantity and quality of Iraq's weapons of mass destruction. Its policies of concealment ensured this. We do know that it has had such weapons, has used them, and remains at work on them," Butler concluded.

Compelling testimony, at least for the committee chair. "One thing is clear: These weapons must be must be dislodged from Saddam, or Saddam must be dislodged from power," Biden said ominously. Of course, he hastily added, the hearings were "not designed to prejudge any particular course of action." But he warned that considerable thought must be given to the American role in Iraq if the United States was to succeed in attacking Iraq and removing Saddam. The hearings were terminated with the desired result having been achieved. From the vaunted halls of legislative power, the so-called peoples house, the legislative branch had spoken. Iraq was a threat, and regime removal was the only course acceptable. We just needed to make sure we did it right.

Having succeeded in taking control of the Senate, the PNAC posse moved on to the House of Representatives, where similar "hearings" were scheduled in the days following President Bush's September 12 appearance before the United Nations. Following the precedent set by the Senate Foreign Relations Committee, the junior partners in the House stacked the witness list with ringers. One was David Kay, the former nuclear inspector who last served in Iraq in early 1992, just before quitting his post with the International Atomic Energy Agency. "What is clear," David Kay said in his prepared remarks, "is that unless we take immediate steps to address the issue of removing the Saddam's regime from power in Iraq, we will soon face a nuclear armed and emboldened Saddam."

"Saddam's own actions to obstruct the efforts of the international community to carry out the removal of his WMD capacity as mandated by the U.N. Security Council at the end of the Gulf War accounts for the uncertainty as to the exact status of that program today," Kay asserted, removing "all doubt about his aim to acquire and enlarge his nuclear, biological, and chemical weapons stockpiles."[13] No one bothered to ask how one can doubt something that hasn't been sustained to begin with.

And then there was the testimony of Richard Spertzel, the former head of the biological weapons team at UNSCOM. His prepared statement was full of the kind of detail that glazes eyes, deliberately so, because for the most part, his statement said nothing. The zingers were all saved for the end. Iraq, Spertzel noted, "has had twelve years to advance its viral capability and . . . this almost certainly includes smallpox as an agent." A stunning assertion, backed up with absolutely no factual data, either derived from his experience as an inspector or from elsewhere. Spertzel simply spoke, and suddenly smallpox as an Iraqi weapon became part of the record, playing off the most base fears of the American public, informed as it had been by the Bush administration that the single greatest threat to Homeland Security lay in a smallpox attack.

But Spertzel had more to offer. "Even more ominous [Author's note: as if something can be more ominous than smallpox.] is Iraq's successful efforts to acquire the necessary equipment and reagents for adding genetic engineering to its [biological weapons] repertoire. This was particularly alarming because, at the same time, key personnel in Iraq's virus and bioengineering [biological weapons] program were no longer functional at their stated work locations." Again, Dick Spertzel injected personal theory as fact. Genetic engineering? Bioengineering? Iraq had no such programs, and yet, thanks to Dick Spertzel, they now did on record. And then the grand finale: "There is no doubt in my mind that Iraq has a much stronger BW program today than it had in 1990. Perhaps of most concern would be anthrax and tularemia bacteria and smallpox virus." After a decade of sanctions, seven years of intrusive weapons inspections, Dick Spertzel believed the Iraqi biological weapons program was stronger today than it was in 1990.

Some in the audience didn't swallow everything without at least chewing on it for a while. Representative Jo Ann Davis (R–Virginia) queried Spertzel on the fact that from his testimony one could draw the conclusion that no concrete evidence concerning the threat of Iraq's weapons capabilities had been produced, or could be produced.

SPERTZEL: "If you're looking for a smoking gun . . ."

DAVIS: "I am."

SPERTZEL: " . . . I can absolutely guarantee you, you will not find it. Not now. Not in the future. The technology for finding that smoking gun, at least in the biology field, is not there. You absolutely will not find it."

DAVIS: "So you could be asking Congress to vote on going into Iraq based on total speculation?"

SPERTZEL: "That's one way of looking at it. I mean, you know, you do an assessment based on the best information. I mean that's the way we finally got Iraq to acknowledge their BW program. It was an assessment of the information. Admittedly sketchy. But it seemed to make a cohesive story. And that's what you have to act on. It is a value judgment. There's no way around it."

War as a value judgement, apparently a concept many in Congress were not willing to contemplate.

On September 26, 2002, the Bush posse began its task of setting Saddam up for the execution. Colin Powell, the much respected secretary of state, came out aggressively during his testimony to the Senate Foreign Services Committee. "Let me just make two points," the one man who served in the administrations of Reagan, the first Bush, Clinton, and the second Bush said to the assembled senators, "we can have debates about the size and nature of the Iraqi [weapons of mass destruction] stockpile. We can have debates about how long it will take [Saddam Hussein] to reach this level of readiness or that level of readiness with respect to these weapons. But no one can doubt two things. One, they are in violation of these resolutions. There's no debate about that. And, second, they have not lost the intent to develop these weapons of mass destruction. Whether they are one day, five days, one year, or seven years away from any particular weapon, whether their stockpile is small, medium, or large, what has not been lost is the intent to have such weapons of mass destruction."

Two points made, neither of which were in doubt. Iraq is in violation of its obligation to disarm, and Iraq intends to possess weapons of mass destruction. No doubt, no debate. And no one asked any questions, or demanded to know why there was such certainty. The Big Lie had been swallowed hook, line, and sinker.

Sure, some senators were uneasy with the whole thing. "Part of our dilemma here," Senator Biden bemoaned, "is that, as I said at the outset, we're being asked to pass a resolution that is broad before the president has made a decision whether or not he is going to go to war. So we're going to give, in effect, under constitutional theory, the equivalent of a declaration of war before the president has decided to go to war. I don't know of any time in American history that's ever been done." Good point, Senator, which was all the more reason to subject the president's man to some harsh questioning on the reasons for war. But Joe Biden had just presided over his own kangaroo court, passing sentence over Saddam and his regime. Why would he stand in the way of the executioner?

Other senators made a pass at the reasons for war. When pressed by Senator Paul Sarbanes (D–Maryland) about the threshold for war—what the United States was willing to fight for—Secretary Powell responded, "The principle reason for the authority is for the president to do what he needs to do to focus on the principle offense he has been presenting to the nation, and that is weapons of mass destruction."

This prompted Senator Kerry to ponder his own dilemma: "If Iraq were pushed to a point that they had to comply, and did comply fully with an unfettered, unconditional spot inspection satisfactory to the new regime [of inspections] which you are seeking from the United Nations, and it was met, would you go to war?"

Powell was forced to give an answer, although he was hesitant to do so. "If Iraq was disarmed as a result of an inspection regime that gave us and the Security Council confidence that it had been disarmed, I think it unlikely that we would find a *causus belli*."

No one brought up the possibility that Iraq might have actually disarmed, that this whole effort by the Bush posse was just a charade, a masterful piece of theater performed before an all too compliant audience willing to believe the illusion.

"If the United Nations Security Council won't deal with the problem," the president stated clearly, "the United States and some of our friends will."

As if Iraq were some unruly outsider at a frat party, and Dubya and the boys were simply cleaning house. The fact of the matter is that any friends we had would be doing us and the world a grave disservice by going along with the president's not-so-little war. When the president spoke of friends, I was reminded of the slogan, "Friends don't let friends drive drunk."

Here we were, America, drunk on power, at the wheel of a foreign policy that threatened to shred the very fabric of international law that has held the world together since the end of the second World War. The unilateralist, America-first-at-any-cost approach of the new "Pax Americana" policy formulation was as dangerous as any eighteen-wheeler careening down the highway with a drunk behind the wheel. The last thing we needed were facilitators to this policy, those who sat by silently while America redefined its role in the world, without any consideration given to other nations.

We needed friends, the real kind, who would step up and confront us, however uncomfortable such confrontation may be, turn the engine off and take the keys away from us. We needed to be reminded that, as a member of the global community of nations, the American voice counts, but it is not the only voice that counts. During the fall of 2002 I crisscrossed Europe, delivering this message where I could. The European Parliament. The Danish Parliament. Sweden, Norway. The Italian Parliament. The message was well received by the people of Europe, but sadly, not by their leadership, who either sided with Team Bush, or chose to sit on the fence.

One of the reasons the message I tried to deliver fell on deaf ears is that the people of the United States were themselves ambivalent. It was hard to motivate Europeans to do something that the Americans seemed unwilling to undertake. This is a family affair, and just like a family that needs to confront a member who is alcohol dependent, America needed to confront its president about this all-consuming quest for power. The strength of American democracy is the people of America, and who better to be friends with than ourselves. We proved to be bad friends indeed.

The PNAC posse had finally succeeded in codifying as official policy the guidelines Paul Wolfowitz had written down over a decade earlier. The "National Security Strategy" document that the Bush administration embraced as official policy in September 2002 was about naked power, plain and simple. It was a rejection of the principles that had guided America as a nation since the time of our founding fathers. It spoke of imposing a "distinctly American internationalism" on the world, leveraging American military and economic power to encourage "free and open societies." Rather than defining a grand "Pax Americana," the National Security Strategy document outlined an "Imperial America," which rejected diversity and promoted confrontation.

And Iraq was to be the first manifestation of this new policy of confrontation.

Iraq as a threat became national entertainment. Like reality television, Americans had only to tune in and they would soon get their fair share of the real-life adventure playing out before their eyes. That this was all a carefully orchestrated fraud and deception apparently never crossed their mind, primarily because, as the reality programming called "Get Saddam" kept telling them, it was Saddam Hussein that was doing all the deceiving. Just ask Victoria Clarke, the Pentagon's tougher than nails spokesperson. On October 8, 2002, she paraded before the assembled Washington, DC press to introduce to the American people a "new" concept: Iraqi denial and deception. Iraqi denial and deception, Ms. Clarke said, is a highly organized and comprehensive program to hide weapons of mass destruction and their development. America should be scared. To back her up, Ms. Clarke introduced Dr. John Yurechko, the Defense Intelligence Officer for information operations and denial and deception at the Defense Intelligence Agency. He was quick to boast about the incredible sources he had assembled to back up the theories contained in his briefing.

"A number of former UNSCOM inspectors, senior UNSCOM officials, and even Iraqi defectors have described this effort in considerable detail," Dr. Yurechko noted. "This body of testimony includes—and I'll give you a few examples—David Kay's famous 1995 article in the *Washington Quarterly*; the British inspector Tim Trevan in his 1999 book, *Saddam's Secrets: The Hunt for Iraq's Hidden Weapons*; several insightful articles and reports by the former U.S. inspector David Albright; former UNSCOM Chairman Richard Butler, in his valuable book, published in 2000, *The Greatest Threat*. And if these western sources don't suffice, there's not a small, but growing, body of accounts by knowledgeable Iraqi defectors. For example, the former Iraqi nuclear scientist Dr. Khidhir Hamza published *Saddam's Bombmaker: The Terrifying Inside Story of the Iraqi Nuclear and Biological Weapons Agenda*. The list, predictably, didn't include the book written by the head of the Concealment Investigation Team who had originated the concept of Iraqi concealment, denial and deception—*Endgame*. No, the author of that book wasn't considered a reliable source by the Defense Intelligence Agency, at least not in public.

Dr. Yurechko noted that the Iraqis, in carrying out their programs of denial and deception, had three objectives: "to blur the truth about Iraqi compliance with their disarmament obligations; to ensure that UNSCOM could not uncover the true full scope of Iraq's WMD programs; and third, to prevent UNSCOM from achieving the complete disarmament of Iraq's WMD."

If I had been invited to speak on the same platform, I would have noted that this statement more accurately described the policy of the United States, which was one of the reasons I resigned from my post as U.N. weapons inspector.

Objective one: blur the truth about Iraqi compliance. Cue slide: "This is an example of a suspected Iraqi biological warfare facility," Dr. Yurechko said, speaking to his script. "Take a good look at the picture. One of the interesting features of this facility is its location. It's in a residential area . . . the buildings are nondescript in nature . . . the issue for us today is how many undetected BW facilities of this type exist . . . if they are undeclared and undetected and concealed WMD sites, by definition they cannot be inspected or monitored. And the inspection regime cannot provide any level of assurance that a country is not conducting illicit activities."

Did they or didn't they disarm? No, Dr. Yurechko said, and the evidence to support this is Iraq's submission of fraudulent declarations to the inspectors. Evidence? "Richard Butler, the then UNSCOM Chairman, stated that Iraq's September 1997 BW declaration, quote, "failed to give a remotely credible account of Iraq's biological weapons programs.""

Except we now know that Iraq in fact did submit an accurate report, 12,500 pages worth of data which have yet to be contradicted by any findings of the U.S. military in the course of their search for weapons in Iraq.

Objective two: ensure UNSCOM could never uncover the truth. By "sacrificing certain elements of WMD programs," Dr. Yurechko noted, "Baghdad has tried to generate a public impression of cooperation while working hard to conceal essential information on the scope and capabilities of its WMD programs." Key to this deception, according to Yurechko, were so-called dual use facilities used by Iraq for concealing weapons of mass destruction production and impeding inspections. "All components and supplies used in WMD and missile programs are dual-use. For example, any major petrochemical or biotech industry, as well as even a public health organization, will have a legitimate need for the materials and equipment that can also be used to manufacture some chemical and biological weapons."

Translation: The whole country was dual-use.

Objective three: prevent UNSCOM from doing its job. Evidence? Presidential palaces. Radwaniyah, a particularly big one, was cited, some eighteen square kilometers ideally configured to be "an integral part of the Iraqi concealment effort designed to hide their weapons program materials." No data was submitted to back up this assertion, just the statement itself. Of course, today Radwaniyah is under the total control of U.S. occupation forces, and nothing remotely resembling an "integral part" of a concealment effort has been found.

"Who are we to believe is telling the truth?" Dr. Yurechko asked the journalists. "What are we to believe is the truth?"

Good questions. Who to believe? Not Dr. Yurechko, or anyone associated with the Bush administration. What to believe? Anything but what is put out by the Bush administration. The sad fact is that, on the issue of Iraq's disarmament, a brutal dictator named Saddam Hussein has proven to be more truthful than the elected government of the people of the United States. That, more than anything, is a true mark of how low Sheriff Bush and his PNAC posse have brought us.

The "Get Saddam" reality television show maintained its steady stream of on-message programming. On the same day as Dr. Yurechko's presentation, Americans were enthralled by the words of their commander in chief, who articulated the threats posed by the Iraqi dictator and his weapons of mass destruction. "The danger to America from the Iraqi regime is grave and growing," Sheriff Bush said grimly. "In defiance of pledges to the United Nations, Iraq has stockpiled biological and chemical weapons, and is rebuilding the facilities used to make more of those weapons . . . we cannot leave the future of peace and the security of America in the hands of this cruel and dangerous man. This dictator must be disarmed . . . I urge Americans to call their members of Congress to make sure your voice is heard. The decision before Congress cannot be more consequential. I'm confident that members of both political parties will choose wisely."[14]

But first the Sheriff needed an arrest warrant. President Bush turned to Congress and asked them to complete the final act of what had become the tragic abrogation by the people's elected representatives of the Constitutional responsibilities that had been entrusted to them—give the president absolute war powers authority even before he has gone public with his decision to go to war. And Congress did his bidding, the House of Representatives voting 296–133 in favor, and the Senate voting 77–23 in the same manner.

Some Senators, like Delaware's Joe Biden, pretended that this wasn't a war vote. Biden said he backed the resolution "because we should support compelling Iraq to make good on its obligations to the United Nations . . . a strong vote in Congress increases the prospect for a tough new U.N. resolution on weapons inspections, which in turn decreases the prospects of war."

Others, like Mississippi's Trent Lott, were more honest, noting that the resolution "will lead to a safer world," setting in motion "the beginning of the end of Saddam Hussein and all he stands for."

And some, like Massachusetts's John Kerry, simply couldn't make up their mind. "Regime change," he said, "has been an American policy under the Clinton administration, and it is the current policy. I support the policy. But regime change, in and of itself, is not sufficient justification for going to war, particularly unilaterally, unless regime change is the only way to disarm Iraq of the weapons of mass destruction pursuant to the United Nations resolution. As bad as he is, Saddam Hussein the dictator is not cause for war. Saddam Hussein sitting in Baghdad with an arsenal of weapons of mass destruction is a different matter."

On October 16, 2003, the president signed the resolution giving him total control over the decision to go to war with Iraq. "With this resolution," he stated, "Congress has now authorized the use of force. I have not ordered the use of force. I hope the use of force will not become necessary. Yet, confronting the threat posed by Iraq is necessary, by whatever means that requires. Either the Iraqi regime will give up its weapons of mass destruction, or, for the sake of peace, the United States will lead a global coalition to disarm that regime. If any doubt our nation's resolve, our determination, they would be unwise to test it."

Most Americans were blind to what had just transpired. The reality television programming was simply too riveting, too entertaining, for them to actually believe any of this was, in fact, real. And when someone dared speak up in objection, well, that deviated programming's script, and as such was tuned out. One has to wonder if the faith in the American people Senator Robert Byrd (D–West Virginia) expressed while lamenting the decision to give the president war powers authority was well placed.

"Were I not to believe in the inherent ability of the Constitution to withstand the folly of such actions as the

Senate is about to take," Senator Byrd said, "I would not stop fighting. I would fight with every fiber of my body, every ounce of my energy, with every parliamentary tool at my disposal. But I do believe that the Constitution will weather this storm. The Senate will weather the storm as well, but I only hope that when this tempest passes, senators will reflect on the ramifications of what they have done and understand the damage that has been inflicted on the Constitution. In this debate, the American people seem to have a better understanding of the Constitution than those who are elected to represent them. Perhaps it is that their understanding of the Constitution is not filtered through the prism of election year politics. For whatever reason, I believe that the American people have a better understanding of what the Senate is about to do, a greater respect for the inherent powers of the Constitution, and a greater comprehension of the far-reaching consequences of this resolution than do most of their leaders."

Do we? Only time will tell.

Chapter Six **The Final Case for War and the Sacrifice of Colin Powell**

> "The difference between a moral man and a man of honor is that the latter regrets a discreditable act, even when it has worked and he has not been caught."
>
> —H. L. Mencken

"The United States will ask the U.N. Security Council to convene on February 5th [2003] to consider the facts of Iraq's ongoing defiance of the world," Sheriff Bush told the American people during his January 28, 2003, State of the Union address. "Secretary of State Powell will present information and intelligence about Iraq's illegal weapons programs; its attempts to hide those weapons from inspectors . . . we will consult, but let there be no misunderstanding: If Saddam Hussein does not fully disarm, for the safety of our people, and for the peace of the world, we will lead a coalition to disarm him."

And so it was that the one senior member of the Bush administration's national security team who was not a card-carrying member of the PNAC posse became corrupted. Why he allowed himself to be so degraded is only a question Colin Powell can answer himself, but one thing is certain: far from being his "Cuban Missile Crisis moment," a replay of Ambassador Adlai Stevenson's famous showdown with Soviet Ambassador V. A. Zorin where U-2 photographs exposed the dangerous duplicity of the Russians in irrefutable fashion, Colin Powell's February 5, 2003, date with destiny will go down in history as his time of shame, the moment in which, in a flash of duplicity, an entire career's worth of service and credibility was erased.

It certainly didn't start off as such. Indeed, in the aftermath of his presentation, many believed that Colin Powell had actually pulled it off. But this was more self-deception than fact. The truth is, there was nothing irrefutable about Powell's presentation. We may have suspected it at the time; we know it now. And it is painful, indeed, to go over the transcript of his presentation armed with what we now understand to be the truth. Powell, in introducing his presentation, drips deceit right from the start, noting that one of his main reasons for briefing the council was to provide them with "what the United States knows about Iraq's weapons of mass destruction." He noted that the Bush administration was "providing all relevant information we can to the inspection teams for them to do their work." Well, not really so. We now know that the U.S. held onto the best sites for exploitation by

U.S. Special Operations Forces in the opening moments of Operation Iraqi Freedom, sites that turned out to be empty, but nevertheless had not been shared with the U.N. weapons inspectors. Why risk the lives of military men when the inspectors could have done the job? The presentation to the Security Council was initiated with a lie.

And the lies continued.

"The material I will present to you," Colin Powell told the council, "comes from a variety of sources. Some are U.S. sources. And some are those of other countries. Some of the sources are technical, such as intercepted telephone conversations and photos taken by satellites. Other sources are people who have risked their lives to let the world know what Saddam Hussein is really up to. I cannot tell you everything that we know. But what I can share with you, when combined with what all of us have learned over the years, is deeply troubling. What you will see is an accumulation of facts and disturbing patterns of behavior. The facts on Iraqis' behavior—Iraq's behavior—demonstrate that Saddam Hussein and his regime have made no effort—no effort—to disarm as required by the international community. Indeed, the facts and Iraq's behavior show that Saddam Hussein and his regime are concealing their efforts to produce more weapons of mass destruction."

According to Secretary Powell, the Bush administration placed the burden of proof squarely on Iraq when it came to proving that it has no prohibited weapons. But how does one prove a negative? Iraq had declared that it no longer possesses weapons of mass destruction, and that everything had been destroyed. And with regard to defectors, everyone seems to be loath to discuss the words of the ultimate defector, Saddam Hussein's son-in-law, Hussein Kamal, who repeatedly told his questioners after his August 1995 defection, U.N. and U.S. alike, that in regards to Iraq's weapons of mass destruction, "nothing remains . . . I ordered everything destroyed."

Biological weapons? "Nothing remains . . . all has been destroyed."

Chemical weapons? Ballistic missiles? Nuclear? "All has been destroyed."

That is one defector report that wasn't part of Secretary Powell's report to the Security Council. Instead, Powell misrepresented the Kamal defection, as did the president and vice president before him. "It took years for Iraq to finally admit that it had produced four tons of the deadly nerve agent, VX," Powell said. "A single drop of VX on the skin will kill in minutes. Four tons. The admission only came out after inspectors collected documentation as a result of the defection of Hussein Kamal, Saddam Hussein's late son-in-law." Except Kamal said no such thing. The VX program, like the biological weapons program, was uncovered by the hard work of U.N. weapons inspectors, not the magic wand waving of any single defector. The U.S. government knew this, and Powell should have too.

"Iraq declared 8,500 liters of anthrax," Powell crowed, "but UNSCOM estimates that Saddam Hussein could have produced 25,000 liters. If concentrated into this dry form, this amount would be enough to fill tens upon tens upon tens of thousands of teaspoons. And Saddam Hussein has not verifiably accounted for even one teaspoonful of this deadly material." There was no evidence that Iraq ever produced the cited amount of anthrax; the number Powell quoted is simply an extrapolation, one that Iraq was held accountable to. But this figure failed to take into account the following: Iraq procured the growth media in question in the late 1980s, and it had a shelf life of five to seven years. The last known batch of anthrax manufactured by Iraq was in 1991, and the factory used by Iraq to produce anthrax was destroyed, together with its associated production equipment, under U.N. supervision in 1996. Iraq only produced liquid bulk anthrax, which under ideal storage conditions has a shelf life of three years before it germinates and becomes useless.

Intensive monitoring inspections of Iraq's biological research and manufacturing base carried out from 1995 until the end of 1998 failed to detect any evidence of a retained biological warfare capability. For Iraq to have a viable anthrax stockpile, it would have needed to develop a new manufacturing base since 1999. And the UNMOVIC inspection regime under Hans Blix found no evidence of such a capability. Further more, Iraq has never been shown to have perfected the technique needed to produce the dry powder form of anthrax so graphically presented by Colin Powell when he held up his vial of simulated white powder. Only the United States Department of Defense has, which of course was the source of the anthrax used in the October 2001 letter attacks mentioned by the secretary of state.

Except he left that detail out.

The Iraqi threat painted by Colin Powell was not real, but a phantom menace, something conjured up with smoke and mirrors disguised as "irrefutable fact." How else does one explain the existence of a 1,200 kilometer missile that had never been designed, built, or tested? This part of the presentation was clearly geared toward fear-mongering, an effort to pressure Russia and others ostensibly in the range arc of the Iraqi phantom missiles into supporting a military strike against Iraq.

The entire Powell presentation was a farce, filled with satellite pictures that show nothing, but claim to show everything. During my time as a weapons inspector, the United States repeatedly provided so-called evidence of this nature, displaying photograph after photograph ostensibly showing Iraqi evacuation operations in response to U.N. inspection activity. On two occasions, one in Baghdad and the other in Tikrit, inspectors were able to show that the vehicular activity in question actually related to the gathering and distribution of food supplies. On all other occasions the imagery in question was so vague as to make any definitive judgment impossible. In every case, Hans Blix and his inspectors were able to travel to these sites and conduct a forensic investigation to determine what, if anything, actually took place. Of course, Colin Powell failed to mention that the U.N. inspectors had done exactly that at the nearly one dozen "high priority" sites designated by the CIA, and turned up nothing.

"Here," said Powell, the picture of credibility as he displayed a surveillance photograph to the Security Council, "you see fifteen munitions bunkers in yellow and red outlines. The four that are in red squares represent active chemical munitions bunkers. How do I know that? How can I say that?" Powell had the answers:

> Let me give you a closer look. Look at the image on the left.
> On the left is a close-up of one of the four chemical bunkers.

The two arrows indicate the presence of sure signs that the bunkers are storing chemical munitions. The arrow at the top that says security points to a facility that is the signature item for this kind of bunker. Inside that facility are special guards and special equipment to monitor any leakage that might come out of the bunker.

The truck you also see is a signature item. It's a decontamination vehicle in case something goes wrong. This is characteristic of those four bunkers. The special security facility and the decontamination vehicle will be in the area, if not at any one of them or one or the other, it is moving around those four, and it moves as it needed to move, as people are working in the different bunkers.

So sure of himself. And so wrong, at least according to a German weapons inspector from UNMOVIC who had actually visited the site in question. Peter Franck, the inspector in question, told *Der Spiegel* magazine that he and his fellow inspectors had determined that the vehicles pointed out by Powell as "signature items" were in fact nothing but fire trucks, and that the U.S. government knew this when Powell made his pitch for war.

And then there were those intercepted conversations. I ran the United Nations communication intercept program against Iraq from 1996 to 1998, and experienced several intercepts of this nature. Who are the individuals in question? Do we have full names? What are their affiliations? What call signs did they use? Was this an encrypted conversation, or conducted in the open? Were they operating on military frequencies? Frequencies assigned to security units? Frequencies assigned to personnel responsible for inspection-related activities? How do we know this conversation relates to inspection activity? These are questions that I and my team of communication intercept specialists dealt with all the time, and as a result we were able to sort through conversations that were relevant, and those that were not.

Without additional input from the United States, it is impossible to assert that these intercepts meant anything at all, although Colin Powell asserted they in fact meant everything. If so, then the United States should have provided Hans Blix with the relevant data, allowing the U.N. inspectors to reconstruct the events in question, interrogate the individuals involved, and through forensic investigation determine the relevance of the conversation. But this did not happen.

"The pattern is not just one of reluctant cooperation, nor is it merely a lack of cooperation," Colin Powell told the Security Council. "What we see is a deliberate campaign to prevent any meaningful inspection work." True words, indeed, if Secretary Powell had been honest enough to admit that the nation refusing to cooperate with the inspectors, and working hard to prevent meaningful inspection work, was the United States, not Iraq, because the inspections represented the gravest threat to the war plans of Sheriff Bush and the PNAC posse. Inspections could expose the truth. And truth was the enemy.

"One of the most worrisome things," Colin Powell said to the council ominously, "that emerges from the thick intelligence file we have on Iraq's biological weapons is the existence of mobile production facilities used to make biological agents . . .the description our sources gave us of the technical features required by such facilities are highly detailed and extremely accurate. As these drawings based on their description show, we know what the fermenters look like, we know what the tanks, pumps, compressors, and other parts look like. We know how they fit together. We know how they work. And we know a great deal about the platforms on which they are mounted."

Colin Powell might have been heartened by the discovery, at the end of Operation Iraqi Freedom, of two mobile "laboratories" which the United States claims are the very vehicles briefed by the secretary to the council in February. There is just one problem. They aren't biological labs. At least not according to the most senior British and American experts who assessed them. They aren't configured to produce biological agent; all that could be produced is a thin "broth" which would require significant follow-up processing to concentrate it into something that could remotely resemble agent. The labs lack equipment for steam sterilization, a requirement for making bioweapons. Moreover, there was no ready way to remove the slurry from the alleged fermentation units.[15]

Like the briefing that announced their existence to the world, the American case linking the two discovered "laboratories" to any sort of biological activity is totally without substance. No biological agent has been found. No supporting biological program has been uncovered. No eyewitnesses have been produced to sustain the allegation. On the contrary, the scientists who actually produced the labs say they are used for the production of hydrogen used in meteorological balloons. aluminum, used in the generation of hydrogen, has been found in the so-called fermenter unit. And all experts agree the labs could be used to produce Hydrogen.

The best means of resolving this issue would be to allow impartial and unbiased international experts, preferably operating under Security Council mandate, into Iraq to examine these labs. "We can't think of any other possible use for those two labs," Ambassador John Negroponte stated, rejecting the notion of an independent examination.

Clearly, Mr. Ambassador, we can.

I met Colin Powell once, in September 1998, following my resignation. I had been invited to speak at a gathering of corporate executives in Aspen, Colorado. Mr. Powell was also in attendance. He cornered me in the back of the conference room, where we chatted amicably about Iraq. I reminded him of a passage in his book, *My American Journey*, in which Powell described a situation during the Gulf War where General Norman Schwarzkopf had briefed the press on the destruction of SCUD missiles by coalition aircraft. Powell was confronted by his intelligence chief, who said Schwarzkopf had gotten it wrong. "We don't think these were SCUDs," Powell recorded his intelligence chief as saying to him. "We think they were four Jordanian fuel trucks pulled up at a rest stop." Colin Powell continued the story. "'Where'd you get that?' I asked. 'A captain, an analyst, on Schwarzkopf's staff' came the reply." Powell called Schwarzkopf, and relayed the bad news. The volatile general blew his top and demanded to know where Powell got his data. "'We got the info from your own staff,'" Powell replied. According to Powell, Schwarzkopf was soon back on the phone to him. "'Those certainly were SCUDs,' he said. 'That analyst doesn't know what he is talking about. He's just not as good as the others.'"[16] Powell laughed as I relayed the story. "I'm the captain," I told him. "Well, Norm was wrong about the SCUDs," Powell said, "so I guess he can be wrong about your capabilities." Later, during the question and answer period of my presentation, Colin Powell stood up to sing my praises as a "great American hero" who strove to "speak the truth, regardless of the cost."

As I sat and watched Colin Powell prepare to brief the Security Council, I could only wish he had kept his own counsel. In explaining to General Schwarzkopf why he felt so compelled to intervene on the SCUD issue, Powell pointed out that he was "just trying to protect your credibility. It's a precious asset." Powell chastised himself for failing to correct the record on the false SCUD kill report. "I let the story stand, without correcting it . . . but the truth will out, as it did when a CNN camera crew shot film of the destroyed [Jordanian] vehicles from ground level. Another good media rule: better to admit a mistake than be caught in one."[17]

The truth will out. Don't get caught in a mistake. And yet here was Colin Powell, ready to commit the greatest mistake in his professional career. What we now know, but which was hidden from us on that fateful day in February, was that Colin Powell himself had tremendous doubts about the information he was about to present to the Security Council. I was, Colin Powell noted in September 2002 after I pointed out that the U.S. claims about Iraq's nuclear weapons capability were patently ridiculous, "somebody who is not in the intelligence chain any longer." That may have been true, but my information was much more comprehensive and accurate, as history has shown. Given the deception and manipulation of truth being carried out at the time by the "intelligence chain," I'm certainly relieved not to have been part of it during this dark time in America's history. I would never have stood by silently as lies were perpetrated that I was in a position to correct.

Colin Powell, who was in a position to correct those lies, did not rise to occasion.

"Saddam Hussein is determined to get his hands on a nuclear bomb," Powell told the Security Council. "He is so determined that he has made repeated covert attempts to acquire high-specification aluminum tubes from eleven different countries, even after inspections resumed. These tubes are controlled by the Nuclear Suppliers Group precisely because they can be used as centrifuges for enriching uranium." Colin Powell proudly proclaimed that "all the experts who have analyzed the tubes in our possession agree that they can be adapted for centrifuge use." But we now know that many experts on your own Bureau of Intelligence and Research, together with experts from the Department of Energy (the real experts on centrifuge enrichment) disagreed. So why the lies, Mr. Secretary?

And why didn't you point out to the council as a lie that the other half of your nuclear equation, the alleged attempts by Iraq to procure uranium so loudly proclaimed by the president to the American people during his January State of the Union address, in which he noted that "Saddam Hussein recently sought significant quantities of uranium from Africa." The source of this data? Forged documents provided to the United States by Great Britain. Forged documents given to the British by Italian intelligence services. Forged documents bought by the Italians from a corrupt Niger embassy official in Rome. Forged documents exposed by the United Nations as fakes in less than twenty-four hours. Forged documents Powell himself suspected were forged, which is why he didn't brief that data. But he didn't correct the president. He let the lie stand, just like he let Schwarzkopf's lie stand a decade before.

When confronted with the fact that the evidence cited by the president was, in fact, fabricated, Powell quipped "It [the information] was provided in good faith to the inspectors and our agency received it in good faith, not participating ... in any way in any falsification activities." Powell tried to deflect criticism about his—and the president's—citing of these documents. "It was the information we had," he said to NBC's *Meet the Press* on March 9, 2003, "We provided it. If that information is inaccurate, fine."

No, Mr. Secretary, it's not "fine." Hundreds of Americans died because of that lie, and other lies, told by you and the administration.

You violated one of your maxims learned in Vietnam: "Don't be buffaloed by experts and elites."

Your words were going to send American men and women off to fight and die in a remote corner of the world, just like you and others had been sent to fight and die in Vietnam. Following your Vietnam experience, you promised never again to acquiesce to sacrificing the military in defense of a morally bankrupt policy.

You swore that when it was your turn to call the shots, you'd make sure we never again went to war for "half-baked reasons that the American people could not understand or support."[18]

You knew that the intelligence you were briefing to the council was "half-baked" or, as you are alleged to have said while throwing some of the CIA's paperwork into the air, "bullshit."

You were buffaloed by the experts, Mr. Powell.

You succumbed to the pressures of the PNAC elites.

You failed when your nation needed you most.

The truth will out, Mr. Secretary. And the truth has shown you to be a liar, a moral coward who failed the soldiers, you swore to defend, when they needed you most.

And so we went to war.

Within a month and a half of Colin Powell's fateful appointment before the Security Council, Sheriff Bush ordered American military forces to attack Iraq. The die was cast, the deed done. Powell's presentation created an unstoppable momentum for war. No one dared speak out against the war lest they be called "unpatriotic" or "pro-Saddam." The airwaves were empty of informed dissent. Sure, there were the antiwar demonstrations here in the United States and around the world, but the PNAC posse, together with a compliant media, denigrated and denounced the participants in these marches. One talking head after another was paraded before the American public on the various cable news and major network channels, all of whom parroted the same message: war with Iraq was a righteous cause because of the threats posed to the national security of the United States in the form of Iraq's weapons of mass destruction programs.

Just ask Colin Powell.

And so we went to war.

Those voices of dissent that did manage to work their way onto the television set (primarily entertainers with a strong moral sense of right and wrong, but little understanding of the technicalities of weapons of mass destruction or Iraq) were loudly shouted down by the PNAC posse. Blacklists appeared, and livelihoods were threatened, all because a few chose to exercise their civic duty and Constitutional right to speak out against the war. And one of the few voices with the experience on Iraq, the in-depth knowledge of the weapons of mass destruction, who shared a moral vision of America with those who opposed the war, and who was willing and able to join in the protest, was silenced.

And so we went to war . . .

Chapter Seven The Ugly Politics of
Character Assassination

"Trying times are never the times to stop trying."
—Nancy Otto Boffo

In early January 2003, I was convinced that a new strategy for preventing a war with Iraq was needed, and that the key to the strategy was centered on American public opinion. Although sold to the American public by the White House as a matter of national security, war with Iraq was very much driven by domestic political considerations. By my calculations, as long as President Bush and his advisors believed that they would gain more politically by going to war with Iraq than they would lose by holding back, war was inevitable. With every military deployment to the Middle East, every diplomatic effort expended in building a "coalition of the willing," and every iota of political capital invested on the domestic front building a case for war, Team Bush inched toward that benchmark of momentum I termed "critical mass," beyond which stopping a war was all but impossible. I was concerned that, by mid-December 2002, we as a nation had already crossed the "critical mass" threshold, but unwilling to concede peace as a lost cause, was determined to find a way to reverse the push toward war. To do this, I needed to find a way to have an immediate impact on a wider American audience.

I always viewed a trip to Iraq as a silver bullet, something expended only when there was a real potential for positive results. The September trip to Baghdad to address the Iraqi National Assembly represented such a case. I was beginning to think that the time was rapidly approaching where I would need to fire a similar shot. Briefings by Hans Blix and Mohammed elBaradei to the Security Council were scheduled for January 27, to be immediately followed by President Bush's State of the Union address on January 28. I was very concerned that the promoters of war with Iraq in Washington were preparing a one-two punch built around the perception of Iraqi noncompliance, using the U.N. inspectors' reports as a springboard for an aggressive case for war to be made publicly by the president during his nationally televised bully pulpit session. As with the situation last September surrounding the Bush-Blair "War Summit," the time was right for a spoiling attack to be launched, preempting any momentum for war that Team Bush anticipated would build after the State of the Union address.

Certain that war with Iraq was based upon domestic political considerations, I was of the mind that the only practical way to prevent a war was to create an environment that gave President Bush a politically viable "out" from the war without exposing him to attack from his opponents. Given the pathetic state of the Democratic political opposition in the United States, this opening did not need to be a huge one, just something that Bush and his advisors could latch onto as an alternative to military action. I knew that this was more or less an act of desperation, that in the case of war with Iraq the die had already more than likely been cast, but I wasn't ready or willing to concede defeat at that point.

In formulating my strategy, I picked up on something Ari Fleischer, the White House spokesperson, had said in December: The policy of the Bush administration was regime change in Iraq, but this did not necessarily mean the removal at gunpoint of Saddam Hussein. If Saddam fully cooperated with the United Nations regarding the elimination of Iraq's weapons of mass destruction, then this would signal a change in the nature of the regime, and as such signal regime change. Increasingly, however, the Bush-Blair axis had turned toward making the moral case for war, citing the inherent threat posed to international peace and security by the very nature of the Saddam regime. Given this, "regime change" would have to incorporate more than simple disarmament. Significant political alterations would have to be made in Baghdad, in addition to compliance on the disarmament front, before Team Bush could buy any concept of nonmilitary-induced regime change.

In December 2002 I had been approached by Roger Norman, the Director of the Center for Economic and Social Responsibility, or CESR, about a concept they were pursuing to dispatch of a high profile delegation to Baghdad. This delegation, conceptually designed around the figures of Nelson Mandela and Jimmy Carter, sought to address a wide range of policy issues beyond simple arms control. Roger had sent me a working draft of some of his ideas regarding an agenda for such a delegation, and I had replied with comments that the goals of any such effort should be directed at achieving a political impact in Washington and not on the kind of "feel good" issues normally associated with humanitarian interventions. Now was not the time to be talking about economic sanctions or redressing the wrongs done to the people of Iraq. I did think that a discussion of human rights was useful, but only if it resulted in something tangible. And I believed that, given the context of "regime change," a meaningful discussion on democratization and political reform was paramount. Having fired these comments off, I heard nothing back, and assumed that the project had failed to materialize. Never one to remain idle, I brushed off my old notes, added some new thoughts, and organized them into a concept paper.

My good friend Shakir Alkhafaji, the Iraqi-American businessman who had funded the production of my documentary film *In Shifting Sands* out of his own personal assets, had approached me earlier in January 2003 about making a trip to Iraq, accompanied by American political figures. I had balked at the idea for two reasons. First, I didn't believe that such a trip was worth the effort (any benefits would be quickly offset by the negative press that was to be expected), and second, I felt that my presence on such a delegation would dilute the "Ritter effect" that any trip by myself to Iraq would generate. If I went to Baghdad, it would need to be a media event, similar to what occurred the previous September. This wasn't based upon any need or desire on my part to seek the spotlight, but reflective of the reality that public perceptions here in America were largely influenced by what was shown on television. This reality dictated that something dramatic needed to be done to seize the bully pulpit in order to have the opportunity to influence public opinion. Traveling in the company of marginal politicians was not, in my opinion, such an event.

However, in reviewing the concept paper I had just drafted, I believed that this document contained the seeds of a larger intervention, one dramatic enough to not only justify my traveling to Baghdad, but also one that could potentially seize the imagination of the American public, thus making it politically more difficult for Team Bush to argue for war. I had outlined the mission premise along five basic concepts:

• Given the real prospect of imminent war between Iraq and the United States, this intervention needs to take place as soon as possible, preferably before January 27.

• The intervention needs wide media coverage.

• The intervention needs to broaden the debate about Iraq away from simple disarmament.

• The intervention must provide a politically acceptable escape path for President Bush to extricate the U.S. from the Iraqi quagmire.

• The intervention must be meaningful, yet acceptable to Iraq.

Based on this foundation, I drafted three main issues that I felt would serve as the major elements of "regime change":

Disarmament

The Iraqis are fully cooperating with the U.N. in accordance with Security Council resolutions. This cooperation has included unrestricted access to all sites and individuals requested by the inspectors. The inspectors have not found any substantive evidence of Iraq possessing proscribed weapons. While there are gaps in verification concerning certain critical elements of the Iraq declaration, this does not constitute a breach of Iraq's obligations. Iraq will continue to work with the U.N. inspectors with the goal of reaching a satisfactory conclusion to their work, a finding of compliance, and the lifting of economic sanctions. Iraq will pass in the immediate future national legislation which outlaws weapons of mass destruction.

Human Rights

Iraq will strive to implement domestic policies that are consistent with its obligations as a United Nations member, and in keeping with universally acceptable standards of human rights. For this reason, Iraq will open, under the auspices of the Office of the Presidency, a special human rights office, and invites the Secretary General to dispatch to Iraq the U.N.'s representative for human rights to begin discussions on joint work concerning monitoring and reporting on human rights issues inside Iraq.

Democracy

Iraq is committed to the principles of democracy and reconciliation. Iraq will begin working with outside agencies, including the United Nations, to create the conditions for a free and open election for the Iraqi Parliament in three years time. This will include authorizing the establishment of opposition political parties, including those affiliated with expatriate opposition groups. Iraq will work closely with outside agencies (*i.e.*, the United Nations, the government of South Africa, Nobel Prize winners, *etc.*) to develop programs of reconciliation so that the process of democratization is open to all Iraqis without fear or prejudice.

If Iraq could agree to these three points, and come up with a plan for implementation, I felt that there would be a great case for declaring "regime change" in Baghdad, and thus allow Team Bush to declare victory and walk away from the war. But I also felt that given the complexity of the entire Iraqi problem, the pot might need to be sweetened a bit. So I drafted three more issues which I described as optional:

Diplomacy

Iraq is cooperating fully with the United Nations, and will continue to do so. The current crisis is not between Iraq and the United Nations, but Iraq and the United States. For that reason, Iraq will seek every means to reach out and engage the United States diplomatically so that the concerns of both parties can be resolved bilaterally. Iraq is requesting the re-establishment of full diplomatic relations with the United States, recognizing that this is the best means of interacting between the two interested parties.

Economy

Iraq represents its responsibilities to the world in regards to providing secure supplies of oil at reasonable market prices. Iraq is committed to working within acceptable frameworks to ensure that this occurs. The best way to achieve this is to bring control of Iraq's oil resources to the government of Iraq, thus freeing the government of Iraq to better exploit its indigenous resources. Iraq is ready to work with the United Nations, and leading oil exploration and extraction companies, including those from the United States and Great Britain, to achieve this. Iraq is prepared to guarantee the strategic energy requirements of Europe and the United States once economic sanctions are lifted and the current crisis resolved.

Peace

Iraq commits to a regional peace process that seeks not only to resolve the current crisis between Iraq and the United States, but also establish a framework of stability for relations between Iraq and all of its neighbors. Iraq recognizes the nation of Kuwait and its borders. Iraq renounces war with Iran. Iraq seeks to direct its efforts toward regional economic and political stability, and renounces massive military expenditures that exceed legitimate requirements for self-defense. Iraq will work to resolve the Palestinian conflict, and will accept any resolution to the Israeli-Palestinian crisis that is acceptable for the people of Palestine. Iraq rejects violence as

a means of resolving disputes. Iraq rejects terror and terror-
ism, and will work with the international community to
bring an end to acts of international terror.

Many of these concepts had been laid out in my presentation
before the Iraqi National Assembly last September. All I was
really doing was expanding and repackaging them.

I felt that the delegation would have the best chance for
success if it participated in high level discussions with senior
Iraqi Government officials, including Tariq Aziz, Naji Sabri,
Taha Yassin Ramadan, Amer al-Sa'adi, the new Oil Minister
(Amer Rashid had resigned under less than clear circumstances in mid-January), and, preferably, Saddam Hussein
himself. I proposed the delegation arriving in Iraq around
January 23, with discussions taking place between January 24
and 26. I proposed that a statement be prepared to be read at
a joint press conference to be held at the conclusion of the
meetings, in time for the major news programs in Europe and
the United States on January 26—one full day before the
report of Hans Blix to the Security Council. The joint statement would include Iraq's acceptance of the main talking
points. The idea then was for the delegation and the Iraqi
officials to take questions, helping shape the concept of a
media event. I felt that, given the intensity of focus Iraq was
being given by international and American media, there was
no way such an event, together with its contents, could be
ignored.

I emailed the concept paper to Shakir, who in turn for-
warded it to Tariq Aziz's office. The reply was immediate:
"Come to Iraq, authorities at the highest level view your pro-

posal in a very positive light, and will work with you to achieve the desired results."

The battle for American public opinion had begun.

The week of January 12–18 proved to be one of the most emotionally tumultuous periods of my life, a veritable whiplash of highs and lows jammed into a very constricted period of time. I drove to New York City, where I was scheduled to give a presentation to a group of concerned citizens from the entertainment industry. Ben Cohen, founder of Ben & Jerry's ice cream, was working on raising funds for an anti-war media campaign, and my talk was seen as a way of attracting, educating, and motivating potential donors to the cause. Regardless of my impact, the event was a success, raising a fairly substantial amount of money for a series of televised antiwar advertisements.

Following the fund-raiser, I traveled to 30 Rockefeller Plaza, where I appeared on MSNBC's *Donahue Show* face-to-face for the first time on network television with my old nemesis and former boss, Richard Butler. This show had all the elements of high drama. For years Richard and I had been exchanging barbs over our differences regarding Iraq. In the aftermath of my trip there in September, Richard's comments had become quite sharp, accusing me of fabricating events and lying about my work in UNSCOM. I had for the most part held my tongue, carefully documenting a case that supported the totality of my position, and which exposed Richard as a historical revisionist. Armed with these documents, I was more than ready for the showdown.

After a back and forth in which we both outlined our respective positions, Richard and I got down to the heart of the debate—did Iraq possess weapons of mass destruction or not? "I take strong disagreement," I said to Richard, "with the contention that you *know* that Iraq has weapons of mass destruction.

"Oh, come on, Scott," Richard retorted. "That's on the public record."

The transcript of the show followed the ensuing exchange:

RITTER: Of course it's not. The public record actually says, with all due respect—

BUTLER: You signed the papers to me, when you worked for me, advising me—with all of your intellect and knowledge, you signed pieces of paper to me saying that Iraq has hidden weapons of mass destruction.

RITTER: Never. I signed pieces of paper to you that said we have credible intelligence information that says Iraq has it. And I asked your permission to carry out an inspection. But, understand, it's an investigation. You just made a definitive statement that says you know Iraq has weapons of mass destruction. But, with all due respect, Richard, that is never reflected in any of the documents, even the one you just mentioned.

BUTLER: That's not true. There. He all but called me a liar, something he had been doing for several years now. Only this time I was not going to let him get away with it. I pulled out my folder full of documents, including all of the inspection authorizations Richard had just spoken about.

RITTER: It is true. I have it here tonight. Do you want to go through the document page by page and show the people?

DONAHUE: Well, probably not.

BUTLER: It's absolutely established that Iraq has not accounted for—

RITTER: Bingo. I agree with that, has not accounted for. But that's an accounting issue.

BUTLER: So, where are the 500 shells with mustard in them? Where is the 400 tons of—

RITTER: These are good questions, but do you have evidence that they have it?

BUTLER: Where are the missiles?

RITTER: Do you know they have it for a fact, that they possess it as we speak? Or is the problem that Iraq has provided an accounting that we don't have evidence to back it up, that we can't confirm the Iraqi version of disposition? My point is—

BUTLER: Why are you assuming such a degree of innocence on the part of the Iraqis?

RITTER: Because 200,000 Americans are going to war based upon a perception of a threat. You testified before the U.S.

Senate that Iraq has these weapons. And people listened to you and they gave that credibility, when the fact is, you do not know with absolute certainty that Iraq has these weapons.

BUTLER: Scott, the United States—

RITTER: And I'm not going to stand by and let Americans die in combat because people like you mislead the American Congress. I just won't allow that to happen.

BUTLER: Oh, for God's sake, for God's sake, I mislead the American Congress?

RITTER: You said you know where the weapons are. Where are they?

BUTLER: Please allow me to finish. There is on the record at the United Nations pieces of paper signed by you—

RITTER: I have them here.

BUTLER: —addressed to me, saying, these people have concealed weapons. Please authorize me to go find them.

RITTER: And you signed those documents.

BUTLER: Sometimes I did and sometimes I told you no.

RITTER: Give me an example when you said no.

BUTLER: I told you no because I thought what you were doing was excessive.

RITTER: Give me an example, Richard.

BUTLER: Come on.

RITTER: No, please, in front of the people here tonight. You've said this many times. You've brought my credibility into question. I can document every time we've met, every time I briefed you, and every time you signed it. Please, for the benefit of the public tonight, one example of when you turned me down.

And Richard Butler did not, because he could not. I had him cold, and he knew it. Phil Donahue took the show into a commercial break, and Richard and I sat there, making uncomfortable small talk. I could tell by the look in his eyes that he was not pleased with the direction this conversation was going. I decided to offer an olive branch, and told Richard that I had made my point, and I saw no reason to keep going down this path when the larger issue was war with Iraq. Richard agreed, and took the cue when we came back on air.

BUTLER: Look, I think Scott and I would agree that weapons of mass destruction are bad for people's health.

DONAHUE: We all agree.

BUTLER: OK? And we have to do something about it.

DONAHUE: Right.

BUTLER: I'll tell straight up what my concern is. I have no doubt about the evil that Saddam Hussein constitutes.

DONAHUE: Everybody says—

BUTLER: No doubt that he has weapons of mass destruction that need to be accounted for, and probably made more. But what I am concerned about is that, if we go and attack Iraq on the basis of their weapons of mass destruction, that people will ask, why now? Why this country now? What about the other weapons of mass destruction in the world? Or are you really just about oil or whatever? We have to be a whole lot clearer about the reasons for which we're doing this, given that our record on weapons of mass destruction isn't good enough. Saddam's is one thing. But what about ours? What about other countries?

Remarkably, Richard continued in this vein, and in the end finished with a flourish that echoed much of what I had been saying for some time now.

BUTLER: International law since the second World War in the charter of the U.N., the thing that we all live by, says that every state shall be independent. Every state, country, that is, shall be able to choose its own government. All political disputes must be settled by peaceful means, and it is against the law to invade or attack anyone. The only use of force that is legal is 'A,' in your own self-defense, and 'B,' when the Security Council says that it's OK to defend the peace. Now,

Washington will say that an attack upon Iraq is OK to defend the peace. And this is maybe where Scott and I will join each other. We need evidence for that. We need something better than the simple threat by George W. Bush that says, If you won't do it, we will.

DONAHUE: Right.

BUTLER: That sounds awfully lot like American imperialism to me, and I think that's very dangerous.

I couldn't have stated it any better.

I headed back to Albany the next morning. During this time I was constantly working the phone, trying to put together a delegation that could have credibility on the international stage if and when Iraq committed to the main points of the intervention. Key players like South Africa's Nelson Mandela and Bishop Tutu, and Ireland's Mary Robinson, were unavailable for one reason or another. Denis Halliday, the United Nations former coordinator for humanitarian affairs in Iraq, had just returned from Baghdad, but had expressed his willingness to go back and assist with the intervention. Norman Solomon, the executive director of the Institute for Public Accuracy, which had funded past trips to Iraq by Sean Penn, former Senator James Abourezk, and others, had also agreed to provide fiscal support for the intervention, and was added to the delegation at the last minute to round out the team. Shakir Alkhafaji was coming along as well, serving in the all important role of intermediary and facilitator. Without Shakir, nothing was going to be accomplished.

On January 15, I traveled to Williams College in Williamstown, Massachusetts, where I spoke to a capacity crowd about the coming war with Iraq. It was a solid event, with fantastic questions from an audience composed of students and local citizens alike.

On my way home the next day, I was stunned to hear reports about U.N. weapons inspectors discovering chemical warheads in Iraq. Something had to be wrong, I thought to myself. If this was true, it undermined everything I had been saying about a qualitatively disarmed Iraq, and paved the way for war without any hope of forming a viable opposition. It also scuttled the planned Iraqi initiative before it could even get off the ground.

I went into a defensive crouch upon my return home, pushing aside repeated attempts by Fox News to get me on air to talk about the "discovery." The Fox announcers were openly gloating about the find, and nearly salivated on air in anticipation of the war to come. But after a cursory look at the evidence, I knew this to be a red herring: old 122mm artillery rockets. These weren't even chemical warheads, simply unfilled munitions, purchased in 1986 and long since expired. Iraq was overrun with these munitions. They were accountable under the provisions of U.N. Security Council resolutions, and Iraq had declared and presented tens of thousands of these shells to UNSCOM for destruction. But many remained unaccounted for, destroyed during the massive aerial bombardment of 1991, scattered across the countryside when munitions storage depots detonated in volcanic fury, or simply misplaced when central accounting documents were themselves destroyed by fire and explosion.

UNSCOM inspectors had stumbled across similar weapons several times during our seven-plus years in Iraq—the most recent in December 1997—and never once did we make such a fuss to the press. I was dismayed that Hans Blix was allowing this "discovery" to get so out of control, and was determined to do my part in order to set the record straight.

It was in times such as this that I believed I did some of my best service in the cause of peace and justice. Your average antiwar political activist simply was not equipped with the knowledge and experience to address an issue of this nature. I was, and try as they might, no one could dismiss what I had to say. In rapid succession, I hit the BBC and U.S. radio waves, aggressively responding to the allegations of Iraqi noncompliance and setting the technical case straight on the nature of the munitions involved. I appeared with Neil Cavuto on Fox, the Abrams report on MSNBC, *Crossfire* on CNN, and then back to Fox for Greta Van Sustren's show. In between I did commentary for local television here in Albany, and capped it off with a midnight radio interview with the Australian Broadcast Corporation. The media blitz continued the next day, January 17, with an early morning radio interview with the BBC in London, followed by an appearance on Paula Zahn's *American Morning* on CNN. I was overwhelmed with radio interview requests, and had agreed to do a long interview with the Canadian Broadcast Company at 7.30 P.M. To top it off, CNN was airing the Richard Roth interview I had done back in December on Gulf War syndrome and the Iraqi FFCD documents. My media campaign was getting into full stride, and I believed I was starting to blunt the impact of the outrageous claims being made about the newly-discovered unfilled munitions, not to mention the issue of whether or not Iraq possessed any weapons of mass destruction at all.

Suddenly, without any advance warning, things came crashing to a complete halt. In the midst of doing interviews on Thursday, January 16, I had received a telephone call from Special Agent Beth Gallagher, the senior investigator for the FBI's National Security Division in New York. I had not spoken with the FBI since the spring of 2002, but given the amount of phone calls I had been making on my cell phone about the Iraq initiative, together with the related email traffic, I wasn't surprised to find the FBI newly energized about my case. Beth wanted to meet, and soon—before I left on my trip. While I had no real desire to have anything to do with the FBI, I stuck to my philosophy that since I knew I was doing nothing wrong in the eyes of the law, the best way to diffuse the FBI's attentions was to deal with their concerns head-on. I agreed to a meeting at 10:30 A.M. on Friday, January 17, at a local Marriott Hotel room the FBI would book for the occasion. Beth told me the meeting should last for at least two hours, maybe more.

The meeting went well. Beth was joined by a second agent, Nick Panagakos, whom I had met before in New York City, and they grilled me about my September 2002 visit to Iraq, how it was organized, who funded it, who I met, what my motivations for going on the trip, *etc.* The FBI was very interested in my personal finances, and how I was sustaining myself during this period of activism. They seemed to have no trouble accepting the fact that I could make a living from public speaking and writing. They spent the last half of the meeting querying me about my upcoming plans to travel to

Iraq and what I hoped to accomplish. The meeting ended with both Beth and Nick wishing me the best of luck, and asking that I contact them when I returned from Baghdad. (In keeping with the surreal atmosphere of these meetings, we parted with me signing a few copies of *Endgame* for other FBI agents in the National Security Division who couldn't attend the meeting.)

I returned home and immediately fell into the drill of answering the never-ending phone calls from radio stations around the world requesting interviews. And then it came— *the* phone call. A reporter from the *Schenectady Gazette,* wanting me to comment on a story they were going to run on the front page of Saturday's paper concerning my arrest in June 2001 by the Town of Colonie Police Department on Class-B misdemeanor charges. I was stunned—with all that was going on, this was the absolutely last thing I expected to be confronted with. The case had been dismissed by a judge and the file sealed with the concurrence of the Town of Colonie Police and the District Attorney's office, and I had put the entire episode behind me. I called my lawyers, who were quickly able to confirm that someone had discussed issues allegedly pertaining to the arrest and sealed file, and that the Gazette was going with the story, which centered around allegations by the District Attorney, Paul Clyne, that my case had been improperly handled by the Assistant District Attorney involved, Cynthia Preiser, and that the dismissal was inappropriate. Cynthia Preiser was fired, and the Albany media had a new, juicy scandal to sink their teeth into.

I count myself blessed for the love and support of my family, friends, and colleagues, but throughout my life one person has shone above all others—my wife, Marina. This new test handed to us courtesy of the *Schenectady Gazette* (and those who orchestrated the timely leak of the dismissed case) proved to be no exception. Marina and I discussed this new challenge, and while I was prepared to stay home and confront this issue head on, Marina pushed me to keep to my travel schedule, which meant hitting the road first thing Saturday, January 18, the same day the story broke. I flew to Los Angeles and spoke to a packed venue of over 2,000 people in Claremont. I continued on to San Diego, speaking to the major local media outlets as well as a group of over 100 at a book signing. News travels slowly, and no one raised the issue of the arrest during the trip. Back at home, things were different. Marina had to deal with media stakeouts, with television crews lurking outside our home, trying to get an interview. This was exactly the sort of thing I didn't want Marina to deal with alone. But despite my desire to return home and deal with the media, Marina demanded that I stay on course with my schedule. So I flew to New York City, where I filmed one of the Ben Cohen television spots and prepared for my flight to Amman, Jordan.

But the trip wasn't meant to be. Norman Solomon, under pressure from his staff at the Institute for Public Accuracy, was balking at going to Iraq if I was a participant. If Norman fell out, funding for Denis Halliday would disappear as well, meaning that I would be flying solo with all of this negative press serving as a major distraction. I spoke with Denis, and while he was disturbed that I was not going, and doubted the initiative could succeed without my presence, he agreed to continue on the mission together with Norman Solomon and push for the best. I called Shakir and explained the situation, and he agreed to help out with the Norman-Halliday visit as best he could, but likewise expressed dim hopes for a break-through without me along.

Back home, I took the media head on. After consulting with my lawyers, we agreed that the best strategy was to stick with the facts, emphasizing that while there had been an arrest, the case had been reviewed in court, and that the judge, together with the police and the assistant district attorney, agreed to a dismissal, thus nullifying the arrest. The file was sealed, something done on the order of the judge to protect all parties involved from unsustained allegations pertaining to the dismissed case (key to this is the requirement, binding by law, on all parties involved not to discuss or allude to any aspect of a sealed file.) The matter was closed. For it to be raised anew at this late date was extremely suspicious, something I pointed out over and over. I did a series of local television appearances, then Court TV with Catherine Crier, and finished the news blitz with CNN's Aaron Brown on News Night. It was here that the media showed its true colors. Ignoring the concept of a dismissed case, and brushing aside the legalities surrounding a sealed file, Aaron Brown attempted to carry out what amounted to an extrajudicial proceeding, misrepresenting the law and insisting that I had no choice but to speak about the issue of the arrest and the sealed file, or else be banned from the airwaves as "radioactive." Aaron Brown, CNN, and the rest of the corporate-controlled media had been played like a fine-tuned fiddle by those who had leaked the story. Having failed miserably over the course of the past four-plus years to silence me, the anti-Ritter crowd thought they had finally achieved their goal.

There was one problem: I refused to play the game. Rather than crawl into a shell and hide, I continued to press forward. I maintained a robust schedule of public speaking appearances, never dodging the issue of the arrest, but keeping the focus of the discussion where it should be: the coming war with Iraq. I traveled to Japan, where I spoke to members of the Japanese Parliament, the Foreign Correspondents Association of Tokyo, Tokyo University, and a host of media outlets. The issue of the dismissed arrest was never once raised. From Japan I flew to the United Arab Emirates, where I gave a lecture at the Zayed Center, a policy analysis forum underwritten and supported by the government of the U.A.E.. From the U.A.E. it was back to the United States, and a whirlwind of travel that had me speaking in five states in ten days. My downtime was filled with requests for interviews with the foreign press, all of whom were concerned about the looming war with Iraq. Not a single request for an interview came in from any of the major U.S. television networks.

The month of March, 2003, was the same—public speaking at colleges and universities, and trips abroad to France and Canada, where my antiwar viewpoints were given wide coverage. As the United States inched ever closer to war with Iraq, the embargo by the major American television networks continued on the one vocal critic of the war who could effectively counter the allegations of Iraqi weapons of mass destruction that were used by the Bush administration to support its case for war. Finally, on March 19—war. Operation Iraqi Freedom had begun.

Sometime in early April, I started receiving phone calls from the producers of various network shows. "Scott," they would say, "we're interested in having you come on to discuss Iraqi weapons of mass destruction." I would agree, but first ask what the basis of the story was. "We would like you to comment on the reports coming out of Iraq that U.S. forces have uncovered chemical weapons," or something to that effect. I would always agree to do the interview, and invariably the producers would call back—"The interview is off . . . the story turned out to be bogus." I would respond by asking why isn't the story the fact that the U.S.-led coalition was *not* finding any weapons? "That's not the story we're doing right now," the producer would invariably say after an uncomfortable pause. This process repeated itself over and over as more weapons "discoveries' were made—and shown to be false. The "discoveries" got front-page, lead story attention. Their eventual uncovering as unsubstantiated rumor got page eight treatment, if mentioned at all. Having bought into the Bush administration's position that Iraq had these weapons of mass destruction, the media just didn't want to focus on the emerging possibility that maybe these weapons didn't exist, that the whole thing had been a set up.

To the decision makers in today's corporate-controlled media, this wasn't a story.

But it is a story. In fact, the *only* story here is how Team Bush lied to the American people and got the United States embroiled in a war that violated international law. Every headline in America should be highlighting the words in bold print, "Where are the weapons, Mr. President?" Every news program on television should do the same: "Where are the weapons, Mr. President?"

When Secretary of Defense Donald Rumsfeld disseminates, as he did before the Council for Foreign Relations in New York City on May 27, 2003, that the reason no weapons have been found in Iraq by the forces he commands is because it is "possible that they [Iraq] decided that they would destroy them prior to a conflict," he should be answered with scorn and dismay, hounded by the reality that just under a thousand Americans were killed or maimed, together with thousands of Iraqis, on the certainty of knowledge, as Rumsfeld had insinuated prior to the war, that these weapons did in fact exist. A verbal vanishing act simply fails to cut the mustard. There must be an accounting.

"Where are the weapons, Mr. Secretary?"

"It will take time," the secretary of defense said. But how much time?

In the weeks following the fall of Baghdad, my phone started to ring with a different sort of request from the media—they wanted to talk about the fact that the U.S.-led coalition was not finding any weapons. Not just international media—although the British seemed to be more keen than their American counterparts—but also mainstream American cable television news programs on CNN, CNBC, and MSNBC (Fox News continued to be the sad exception) were starting to delve into the exaggerations and distortions promulgated by their government's prewar threat assessments of Iraq's weapons of mass destruction. Print outlets like the *New York Times, Newsweek,* and *Time* magazine were beginning to harshly question the failure of Sheriff Bush and his PNAC posse to find any evidence of a crime to justify their lynching of Iraq. The British Parliament and the American Congress began to talk about hearings on the matter. Sheriff Bush and his compliant international deputy, Tony Blair, were in hot water.

Substance had triumphed over smear. The ugly politics of character assassination had failed. While the message had turned out to be more important than the messenger (as should always be the case), it just so happened I was the best conduit for this particular message to be told. And it is a message that must be told, one that screams for an answer:

"Where are the weapons, Mr. President?"

Let the accounting begin.

Chapter Eight **The ABC's of Restoring the American Democratic Republic**

"Democracy is a device that ensures we shall be governed no better than we deserve."

—George Bernard Shaw

"These are the times that try men's souls." This phrase, penned by Thomas Paine in 1776 as the opening line in a series of pamphlets titled *The American Crisis*, addressed the beginning of the American Revolution, our nation's war for independence from British tyranny. The passage of time has altered neither the eloquence nor the relevance of those words, as today the people of the United States face times that are as trying as any we have experienced before. There is an ongoing struggle here in America for the very soul of the nation, one that pits a dangerous cabal of neoconservative ideologues against two centuries of American democracy. It is a struggle fought both in secrecy, behind closed doors, and in the open, waged before our eyes. What makes this struggle so very dangerous is that most Americans are unaware that it is taking place. Battles over fundamental principles and values that define us as a nation are disguised as "bureaucratic exercises" and "politics as usual." But there is nothing normal about what is occurring—the death of a nation for the self-interest of those who would corrupt the very cause of liberty championed by the people.

Americans need to come face-to-face with the definitions of two words—"oligarchy" and "fascism." Oligarchy is a form of government in which a few people have all the power. Fascism is a system of government in which property is privately owned, but industry and labor are regulated by a strong national government, and all opposition is rigorously oppressed. Compare and contrast those terms with the following definitions: democracy, a form of government that is run by the people who live under it, and republic, a nation or state in which the citizens elect representatives to manage their government. America was founded on the principles that define a democratic republic; the America of today has drifted dangerously close to oligarchy, and if not stopped, runs the risk of becoming a neo-fascist state run by PNAC ideologues in concert with their corporate power brokers.

Benito Mussolini, the founder of modern fascism, was brutally honest and to the point when he defined the concepts he embraced. Fascism, he noted "believes neither in the possibility nor the utility of perpetual peace. It thus repudiates the doctrine of Pacifism . . . war alone brings up to its highest tension all human energy and puts the stamp of nobility upon the peoples who have courage to meet it. The foundation of fascism is the conception of the State, its character, its duty, and its aim. Fascism conceives of the State as an absolute, in comparison with which all individuals or groups are relative, only to be conceived of in their relation to the State . . . for Fascism, the growth of empire, that is to say the expansion of the nation, is an essential manifestation of vitality, and its opposite a sign of decadence."[19]

When one compares Mussolini's definition with the "Statement of Principles" espoused by the Project for a New American Century, the parallels are chilling indeed. The latter focuses on defense as the center piece of a strategy that will "maintain American security and advance American interests in the new century," pushing a plan that rejects "short-term commercial benefits" that threaten "to override strategic considerations," a plan that builds on military power as the primary means of "preserving and extending an international order friendly to our security, our prosperity, and our principles." To rely on the military to "preserve and extend" an "international order" is just another way of promoting perpetual war, a not too subtle means of embracing Mussolini's rejection of "perpetual peace," in support of the growth of an American empire that "expands" our nation and "manifests our vitality" in ways that would have done the Italian dictator proud. The eerie resemblance of the concept of a "New American Century" as promoted by the PNAC posse to Adolf Hitler's "Thousand-Year Reich" should send chills down every person's spine, American and non-American alike.

The PNAC is quick to refute such apt comparisons. William J. Bennet, a signatory to the PNAC "Statement of Principles" and a leading member of the PNAC posse, writes that "with Saddam flouting international law, and President Bush and Prime Minister Tony Blair attempting to enforce it, portrayals of Bush as Adolf Hitler—as we saw and heard in the "human rights" protests—betray an ignorance of liberty, an ignorance of right and wrong, an ignorance of common-sense. Because Bush and Blair are putting together a coalition of countries to oust Saddam, they are labeled the warmongers and tyrants. We live in confusing times indeed."[20]

I agree totally—we do live in confusing times. But the confusion comes not from an ignorance of liberty, right and wrong, and commonsense among those who protest America's faltering off the foundation of a democratic repub-lic and down the path toward oligarchy and fascism, but rather those who are pushing us in that direction—the likes of William J. Benet and the PNAC posse with whom he rides. It is standard practice in the promotion of fascist ideology to point a finger at others and charge them with the very actions being perpetrated by the accuser. Hitler did this in proclaim-ing Poland a threat before ordering his troops to march to Warsaw. Bennett used the same tactics when he spoke of Saddam's flouting of international law while defending an even more egregious violation of those laws by Bush and Blair. It is in keeping with the needs of those promoting fas-cist rule to rigorously oppress those who oppose them. Confusion reigns supreme, and out of this confusion emerges the conditions under which the neo-fascists who seek to impose their "vision" of America on the world can implement their plans.

Bush as Hitler? Maybe not in terms of a point-by-point comparison (we have yet to kill six million Jews, but we are racking up an impressive number of Muslims, including the one and a half million that have died of starvation and disease during the decade of U.S.-led sanctions in Iraq), but the PNAC posse comes dangerously close—too close—to mirroring the fascist model of global domination that Americans and the rest of the world rejected when defeating the Nazi Germany led by Adolf Hitler. Again, we must go to the source, and take a lesson from the words of the original practitioners of fascism, in this case Hermann Goering, who was quoted after his capture, and subsequent trial at Nuremberg, as saying "Why of course the people don't want war . . . that is understood. But, after all, it is the leaders of the country who determine the policy and it is always a simple matter to drag the people along, whether it is a democracy, or a fascist dictatorship, or a parliament, or a communist dictatorship. Voice or no voice, the people can always be brought to the bidding of the leaders. That is easy. All you have to do is tell them they are being attacked, and denounce the peacemakers for a lack of patriotism and exposing the country to danger. It works the same in any country."

It works in America, today, all too well.

Hitler used the events surrounding the burning of the Reichstag on February 27, 1933, as a vehicle for sowing fear in the minds of the German people. Although the actual arson carried out on the seat of Parliamentary government was carried out by units of Nazi storm troopers, Adolf Hitler and Hermann Goering were quick to finger the communists as the culprits, and in less than twelve hours more than 4,000 communists had been rounded up, together with intellectuals and professionals who had opposed the rise to power of the

Nazi party. The German president, Hindenburg, was persuaded by Chancellor Hitler that the German nation was on the verge of a communist revolution, and was pressured to sign an emergency decree which suspended the basic rights of German citizens for the duration of the emergency. The emergency decree expanded the use of the death penalty as a means of punishment, created conditions which denied those arrested the right of a quick trial, access to legal counsel, or the ability to seek redress in the case of a false arrest. Those detained under the emergency decree often had their period of detention extended indefinitely without any sort of legal proceeding. Within a period of little more than a month, Hitler was able to exploit the burning of the Reichstag, and the resultant communist scare, in a manner which enabled him to seize total control of the German state for himself and the Nazi party.[21]

Germany had the Reichstag fire. America had 9/11. While as of yet there is no substantive evidence that shows President Bush and his PNAC posse played a role in facilitating the events surrounding that horrible attack on the United States, there is every reason to believe that this cabal of neoconservatives used the events of that day to sow fear among the American people, paving the way for sweeping changes in the way we as a nation conduct foreign and domestic policy. The resistance shown by the Bush administration to an open airing of the details surrounding the Bush administration's actions before, during and after 9/11 only fuel concern that, while Bush wasn't working hand in glove with Osama bin Laden and al Qaeda, he certainly had all the information necessary beforehand to know such an attack was imminent, and did nothing to stop it. The FBI and CIA had detailed information concerning many of the future hijackers and their intent to do harm, but did little to detain them. The inaction of the Bush administration to the threat posed by Osama bin Laden, combined with the rapidity of the reaction to the 9/11 attacks as far as new policy initiatives and domestic legislation, seems to point to a passive facilitation of the attacks as a triggering event that could be exploited for political gain by Bush and his PNAC collaborators. The Bush administration could try to alleviate concerns of this nature by fully cooperating with the appropriate oversight committees in Congress, but so far has balked at doing so.

The "War on Terror" and the term "terrorist" took on the same tenor and sense of crisis in 2001 America that the concepts of "communist revolution" and "communist" had in 1933 Germany. Sheriff Bush and his PNAC posse rode the wave of fear and ignorance that was generated by the 9/11 attacks to implement an open-ended war on terror, putting in place the condition for perpetual warfare. The war on terror was almost immediately expanded to include not only taking on Osama bin Laden and the al Qaeda terrorists who had attacked America, but the former Afghan freedom fighters turned Taliban militia who ruled Afghanistan, and who had not attacked us in any way. Iraq was put on the list, as were other rogue nations, grouped together in the so-called Axis of Evil President Bush referred to in his January 2002 State of the Union address. Perpetual war for perpetual peace. Orwellian doublespeak.

And then came Attorney General John Ashcroft, whose Justice Department pressured Congress into signing into law the Patriot Act, which gave the federal government sweeping new powers regarding surveillance on American citizens, as well as the ability to arrest and detain Americans. In the aftermath of the war on Iraq, John Ashcroft has lobbied Congress for an expansion of the powers granted to him by the Patriot Act to include expanded use of the death penalty as well as granting the government the ability to hold suspects indefinitely, without legal representation or guarantee of a quick trial. And to guarantee that the American people will not lose focus on the importance of confronting terror, a new Department of Homeland Security was created replete with its own color-coded "mood ring," which in a seemingly arbitrary fashion, sets a standardized "terror alert" to keep the American people at a constant state of heightened tension.

"September 11 changed everything" is the mantra used by the PNAC posse to justify these new, sweeping assaults on civil liberty and the rule of law. But the reality is that the events of 9/11 changed nothing; it is how these events have been exploited by the Bush administration that is making all the changes for the worse in America. The war on Iraq is a case in point. The Bush administration tried its best to tie Saddam Hussein and his regime to Osama bin Laden and al Qaeda, even creating a special intelligence cell inside the Pentagon's Office of Special Projects (OSP, overseen by PNAC posse member Douglas Feith, Undersecretary of Defense for Policy) responsible for culling out from the reams of intelligence on al Qaeda only that data which sustained the allegations of an al Qaeda–Iraq link. The OSP intelligence cell has been alleged to have culled out only that information which sustained the concept of such a link, while ignoring and–or suppressing that which contradicted or debunked the possibility of such linkage.

The OSP cell is alleged to have done the same service in regards to Iraq and weapons of mass destruction. Intelligence generated by this cell was used to brief Congress and the president, and as such influenced policy decision making. No one questioned in any meaningful fashion the work carried out in great secrecy by this cell, in part because to do so would open one up to charges of aiding and abetting the enemy during time of war. The OSP intelligence cell is not unique, but rather part of an overall trend inside Washington to endorse almost without question anything linked with the War on Terror.

While not one to believe in conspiracy theories that have the Bush administration wittingly facilitating the horrific events of September 11, 2001, I do condemn his administration on two counts: first, deliberate neglect of matters of national security in so far as the attacks that occurred on September 11, 2001, were not only predictable, but also preventable, and second, that the Bush administration manipulated the horror of that day in a manner that preyed upon the fear and ignorance of the American people, enabling Sheriff Bush and his PNAC posse to initiate policy, both at home and abroad, which would not have been accepted by Congress or the American people prior to that terrible day. The National Security Strategy and the Department of Homeland Security (with its vehicle of mass mood manipulation, the color-coded "threat alert" system) are but two cases in point. Sweeping assaults on individual civil liberties, the cornerstone of American values, have occurred as a result of the post-9/11 Patriot Act, and further incursions against the American way of life are planned through follow-up legislation. The PNAC posse tells us that "everything has changed" since 9/11, but the only thing that has changed is the consolidation of power within the United States into the hands of a few. There is a huge risk that Bush and the PNAC posse will use 9/11 to do to American democracy what Hitler did to German democracy after the Reichstag fire.

It is our responsibility as citizens to be ever vigilant in defense of our society. This means we should be honest in our evaluation of what is transpiring around us in the name of government. Bush as Hitler? You're damn right. For Americans, Bush is worse than Hitler. Hitler never came close to destroying the American way of life; Bush is accomplishing that objective in spades. Hitler dreamed of global conquest; Bush is doing his utmost to achieve it. The PNAC posse speaks of the dangers of Osama bin Laden, Saddam Hussein, and the other "rogue States," but the sad truth is that Sheriff Bush and his PNAC posse pose the greatest threat to the security of the United States, and international peace and security for that matter, than the world has known for sometime. In typical Orwellian doublespeak, Bush and his posse posture in defense against tyranny, while perpetrating tyranny themselves. They are masters of the Big Lie: America is threatened from dangers that lie abroad. America is threatened, but the danger comes from within, from the very ranks of those whom we elected to protect us.

With the election of George W. Bush the presidency, the PNAC posse found a sheriff they could, and did, manipulate at will, a man with no redeeming qualities, no individual spirit, someone who had spent his life operating in the shadow of a much more powerful (and capable) father, a man who was but a shell, a puppet, waiting to be maneuvered by those with more depth and capability. George W. Bush's record as governor of Texas is only surpassed in incompetence by his record as president, but in both cases his tenure succeeded in empowering an elite few who made their fortunes by manipulating the words and actions of the empty suit holding office. The Big Lie goes well beyond Iraq, weapons of mass destruction, Osama bin Laden, and the war on terror.

Mr. President, you promised the fire fighters of New York City, whose selfless sacrifice you shamelessly exploited for your own political gain, that you would take care of them by providing funds for much needed equipment and training. Where are the resources you promised, Mr. President?

Mr. President, you cravenly exploit the courage and sacrifice of American men and women who wear the uniform of the Armed Forces of the United States, sending them off to fight and perhaps die in one politically motivated adventure after another, and yet you slash the very benefits they will need to sustain them later in life. Where is the budget for Veterans Affairs, Mr. President?

Tax cut? The only tax cuts that have any meaning are those that enrich your already wealthy friends. The rest of us in America will find that the taxes are merely shifted elsewhere, while the federal deficit expands and our national economy collapses. Your economic program is bankrupt, Mr. President, and you are bankrupting the country, too. But you know that, don't you? Like your passive stance toward known threats to the United States prior to 9/11, you are taking a passive stance on the looming economic crisis, because it is in the your interest and the interests of the PNAC posse to have the economic foundations of this nation collapse, enabling you to impose massive reforms that wipe away decades of social welfare programs while preserving and expanding massive defense budgets that dwarf anything required for the legitimate defense of our country. This is the same strategy you used to exploit 9/11, isn't it, Mr. President? You are worse than a liar; you are criminal in your neglect of the nation and the people you were entrusted to lead and protect. You, Sheriff Bush, and the PNAC posse you head up.

Could it be that the president is simply not aware of what is going on? This is not a president encumbered with that "vision thing." He has no vision. He simply isn't smart enough to possess one. He swaggers around, compliantly reading speeches written for him by others, doing the bidding of others, constantly being manipulated by others.

This is not an excuse for his actions, or an attempt to mitigate his personal accountability. Rather, I'm pointing out the need to make sure that, while the president should surely hang—politically speaking—for what he has presided over, there are others culpable as well—the PNAC posse that has bushwhacked America these past years. Their manipulation of the president mirrors that of Hitler getting Hindenburg to bend to his will. The manipulation was made easier by the fact that Bush empowered his manipulators, installing them in the senior-most hierarchy of Washington decision makers from the very beginning. While history may show Bush to have won the presidential election of 2000, at least in terms of the Supreme Court-assisted electoral vote, we should never forget that this president was selected, not elected—and I don't mean the mess down in Florida. I refer to the process in which the PNAC picked George W. Bush as the leader whom they would follow into the White House in the months prior to that election. Tutorials were held in Crawford, Texas, where the president-to-be was carefully schooled on the finer points of the ideology he was to sell to the American people. It's not so much that they wanted him to comprehend the ideology as much as they wanted Bush to be able to sell it in a shallow yet convincing fashion. On the advise of the PNAC, Bush picked Cheney to pick the vice presidential candidate, and Cheney then picked himself (after rejecting a list of so-called viable candidates). Like the proverbial camel who, once getting his head into the tent, soon followed with his entire body, the PNAC posse took full advantage of Dick Cheney's self-appointment to enact a virtual coup d'etat.

With Dick Cheney as vice president, "Scooter" Libby as his chief of staff, Donald Rumsfeld as secretary of defense, and Paul Wolfowitz as deputy secretary of defense, the PNAC posse had a concentration power that was almost unimaginable. Making matters worse, the president, acceding to the will of his underling-masters, kept deputizing more members of the PNAC posse, making the transition from radical neo-conservative ideologue to government official seem frighteningly easy. The president had campaigned on a platform of "compassionate conservatism," a rejection of "nation building," and a foreign policy built on the concept of a "humble" use of American power. But the people he was appointing to the positions of government that would oversee American national security and foreign policy were more like Attila the Hun than adherents to any such pacifist principles.

It is increasingly difficult for me as an American to square the issues of war and the rule of law with the actions of the government of the United States and, by extension, the people it represents, when discussing Iraq. It is one thing to set out ideals and values in a Constitution. It is another to put them into action. More and more, I see the United States heading down the path of expediency when dealing with war and the rule of law. Such expediency is reprehensible to me as an American, representing a deviation from the foundation of beliefs that define America. For me, the Constitution is an absolute; we are not Americans without it. To undertake courses of action at home or abroad which fail to adhere to the principles and letter of the Constitution means that we are turning away from that which defines us as a nation, that which I and others who wear, or wore, the uniform of the Armed Forces are prepared to defend with our lives. I not only revile those who would lead us down such a path, but wonder about those who allow themselves to be so led.

Democracy is not a passive endeavor. It requires an investment of sweat equity by those who seek to prosper within the framework of liberty and freedom that democracy brings. I fear that many in America have come to expect the benefits of being an American without first making the investment of citizenship. We are a nation that has stopped voting. We are a people so accustomed to wrapping ourselves in a cocoon of comfort that we fear anything that rocks the boat of prosperity, even if the ship is sailing toward the abyss. We have ceased being a nation of citizens, and instead become a collective of coddled consumers. We have ceded our role as citizen to those power elites and have become blind to their abuses of power and the destruction of what we stand for as a people—so long as these power elites keep us waddling down the path of relative prosperity. Sheriff Bush and his PNAC posse are the embodiment of such elites, and the path they have us waddling down is the path of our own destruction.

For America to survive, its citizens must rediscover who we are as a people. We must reacquaint ourselves with the Constitution of the United States, and what it means to be an American. We must re-embrace the concepts of citizenship, and the will to do so actively. The urgency of the moment is real, especially in this time of war and fear. Now is the time to ask questions, to demand answers, to hold those whom we elect to represent us accountable for what they do in our name. Such engagement is not only good citizenship, it is the most patriotic thing an American can do in defense of the ideals and values of American democracy. But we must be diligent in our defense of American democracy. We cannot allow ourselves to be distracted or misled by those who use the defense of democracy as a false crisis to promote their own seizure and consolidation of power. The PNAC posse has proclaimed that the best way to defend American democracy is to export its values and principles abroad, and have offered us their vision of a "new American century" as the vehicle to do this.

The basic PNAC premise of exporting American democracy is fundamentally flawed. We can no more successfully export that experience than we can change human nature. American democracy is an expression of a unique American history, and because American history is still evolving, through the very nature of our continued existence,

American democracy is very much a work in progress, an unfinished masterpiece unsuitable for marketing. We are not a dead nation, like ancient Babylon, Athens, and Rome, to be dissected and examined in detail by those seeking to model the development of their own respective societies. We are a living embodiment of our own national will, the will of the people of the United States, and as such are best served by continuing to evolve our society in keeping with the values and ideals set forth by the Constitution of the United States of America. Trying to export this uniquely American experience not only ignores the historical imperatives and realities of non-American peoples, but does a grave disservice to the very principle of self-determination that we espouse to cherish and defend.

We must find it in ourselves to resist the temptations of Empire and all that it brings: power, wealth, and security. History shows us that empires are fleeting; it has been said they all die of the same disease—indigestion. There is no reason to believe an American empire would avoid the same fate. To survive as an American democracy in the model set forth by our founders, we must do something unique in the history of the world—voluntarily reject the mantle of absolute power, because we know that absolute power corrupts absolutely. We know that a nation that is built on a foundation of ideals and values that embrace notions of the rule of law and individual civil liberties cannot survive such corruption. That if we assume the throne of global domination, we may continue to call ourselves Americans, but we will no longer be Americans. The noble concept of American democracy will have been forever lost to the American people and the world. This would be a tragedy, not only for the descendants of those American patriots who shed their blood and expended their intellect in crafting the foundations of the American democratic republic, and the descendants of those people in search of a vision and future who flocked to our shores over the course of two and a quarter centuries to build a new home, but also for those around the world who aspire to their own visions of spiritual and physical prosperity, which while expressed in different forms than our own, benefits from the global fallout from the successful implementation of American democracy.

America is going through a crisis of gigantic proportions. It is a struggle for the ideological soul of the nation. Bush and his posse have set a course for the future that dramatically departs, in words and in action, from the values and ideals set forth by our nation's founders. It is a course that ignores the lessons learned from our own troubled historical development, from revolution to civil war, emancipation, suffrage, world war, labor rights, civil rights, and human rights. Throughout this journey, we have struggled with a changing national identity and built the foundational framework of law which would govern how we as a people would exist and co-exist with others. Our nation's founders—George Washington, Thomas Jefferson, John Adams, James Madison, Alexander Hamilton, John Marshall, and others struggled on how to best formulate the unique blend of federal, state, and individual rights that made America the bastion of freedom and democracy that has, until now, withstood the test of time and trial. Those that followed—Abraham Lincoln, Theodore Roosevelt, Woodrow Wilson, Franklin Roosevelt, Dwight

Eisenhower, and others—built on this body of work, keeping the American dream relevant and viable. The journey from founding to modern times has not been a smooth one, nor has the product that has emerged been free of blemishes, some existent at birth, others developed along the way. But the modern American democratic republic that we, the people of the United States, brought into the twenty-first century was a durable and invaluable contribution to all mankind, and, as such, one worth defending and sustaining.

Thomas Jefferson noted that, "In every free and deliberating society, there must, from the nature of man, be opposite parties and violent dissensions and discords; and one of these, for the most part, must prevail over the other for a longer or shorter time."[22] As Americans, we cannot be afraid of political debate and discourse, no matter how vitriolic it becomes. There must always be room for partisan politics in a democratic republic, and as Jefferson noted, one party will emerge dominant. There will be periods of violent disagreement, and even social unrest, and those who find themselves on the outside will, at times, despair. But, as Jefferson concluded, with "a little patience, and we shall see the reign of witches pass over, their spells dissolved, and the people recovering their true sight, restoring their government to its true principles."[23]

When undergoing a challenge of monumental proportions, there is a tendency among those tested to fall back on their foundation of fundamental values. It is this tendency that holds the best promise for the survival of the American democratic republic. The neoconservative, neo-fascist perversion of American democracy that is the administration of

President George W. Bush has launched a frontal assault on the basic values and ideals of the United States.

Where are our generation's Washington, Jefferson, Adams, Hamilton, Madison, and Marshall? Sadly, the transformation of American society from one which embraced citizenship to one enslaved by consumerism has failed to produce, or at least identify, leaders of such stature. Does this mean we allow ourselves as a people to drift aimlessly, leaving ourselves at the mercy of the more ideologically unified hijackers of American democracy that control the White House?

No.

We hear talk of Jeffersonian democracy, and the by-product of the revolution Thomas Jefferson helped motivate and lead when he drafted the Declaration of Independence in 1776. "This ball of liberty," Jefferson wrote, "I believe most piously is now so well in motion that it will roll around the globe."[24] But this was no call to world empire through military adventure, but rather an observation that America, in leading by example, could inspire peoples around the world to emulate what we had created.

We find ourselves standing at the threshold of total world domination. We possess absolute power—political, economic, and military. None can challenge us and win. None can stop us from assuming the mantle of global hegemony. And yet, the assumption and execution of such power is not the sign of a great nation. Any despot or tyrant could aspire to such an end, and some may achieve it, but those who seek total power will be totally corrupted by that power, and sadly the United States of America will prove to be no exception. If we continue down the path toward world domination, we will cease being the nation our founders framed. We may call ourselves Americans, but we won't be Americans. We will be something else, a distortion, a perversion of something once great and wonderful.

But it doesn't have to be that way. We still have a chance to be the greatest nation in history. To do this, we need to inspire, to lead by example. This is our collective responsibility. We, the people of the United States, must find it within ourselves to repeat, in deeds and in spirit, the actions of our founding father, George Washington, when he summarily rejected the offer by a worshipful nation to become an American Caesar. King George III, upon hearing of this, is alleged to have said "If he does that, he will be the greatest man in the world." We now must find a way to emulate the actions of George Washington, and turn away from the crown of global power that circumstances of history have offered us. If we don't, and we assume the throne of empire, then we shall go down in history as every empire has before us: defeated, a victim of our own greed and ambition. But if we turn away, and set the example for the world by demonstrating in action what our framers spoke of in word, then we will truly be the greatest nation ever. And that is something we as a people should embrace, for ourselves and our children.

We must fall back on our foundation, the Constitution, and reinvigorate ourselves with the vision and spirit of those who forged our nation out of the fire of revolution. The Constitution, as Chief Justice John Marshall so eloquently reminded us in his various opinions, emanated not from a state or states, but from a sovereign people. As such, it is the people who are the sovereign protectors of the Constitution's authority. The preamble of that document makes this so:

"We, the people, of the United States of America." The framers created three separate, but equal, branches of government—executive, legislative, and judicial—all of which act directly on the people. This is our government. They are employed by us, and they are accountable to us.

This is very much a Constitutional issue. Will someone be able to mount a Constitutional challenge to the excessiveness of Sheriff Bush and the PNAC posse? And how would the Rehnquist Court respond to such a challenge? At this time the answers to these questions are unknown, although in the case of the latter, not unknowable. In theory, the deliberate misuse of national security information could be construed as a "high crime" under the impeachment clause of the Constitution. Defrauding the United States is a felony, and the president has certainly done that.

But the best Constitutional recourse available to the American people is that of a free election.

The first step toward declaring our intention to follow in the footsteps of George Washington is to vote George W. Bush out of office. This man has disgraced the office of the presidency, and with it the nation he leads. His PNAC posse, through their global exercise of frontier justice, have eroded the trust and confidence in America that generations of fighting men and women won through their own selfless sacrifice. Sheriff George W. Bush, the man who ran away from his military duties and the obligations he incurred when he accepted his commission in the Texas Air National Guard (and, mind you, he ran away during wartime, an act of cowardice tantamount to desertion), sacrificed the lives of hundreds of brave Americans in an illegal war of aggression fought not for the defense of the American people, but for the exercise of corporate power. He is joined in this criminality by his deputy, Dick Cheney, a man who found service in Vietnam "inconvenient" to his personal ambition, but was willing to inconvenience the lives of hundreds of thousands of American service members by ordering them off to fight—and in all too many cases, die—in a war which empowered corporate America, including Cheney's own former company, Haliburton, while actually putting the American people at greater risk.

What is needed in America is regime change. It is a good policy when applied to brutal, tyrannical regimes that operate outside the framework of law. Regime change. A new American revolution, waged not on the battlefield, but in the election booth. I don't know whom we should vote for, and I have no way of knowing who will emerge from the pack of Democratic challengers to confront Bush on election day. But I do know that on election day, November 2, 2004, we the people have a choice to make. It is a fundamental choice that will determine the direction of our country. It is a choice about restoring the ideals and values of American democracy. Our choice should be guided by the basic ABC's of this new revolution of democratic self-empowerment:

Anything but Bush and Cheney.

We have no excuse for the future course of events for our nation if George W. Bush is re-elected. It is time to run Sheriff Bush and his PNAC posse out of town once and for all, liberating ourselves from their brand of frontier justice and replacing them with persons who endorse the concepts, put into practice, of Liberty and Justice for All.

Notes

1. George Bush and Brent Scrowcroft, *A World Transformed* (Knopf, 1998) p. 489

2. James A. Baker, III, *The Politics of Diplomacy* (Putnam, 1995) p. 441

3. Colin Powell, *My American Journey* (Random House, 1995) p. 527

4. Anthony Lake interviewed on the Worldnet *Dialogue* program, United States Information Agency, June 30, 1993

5. Project for a New American Century website, www.newamericancentury.org, introductory statement by William Kristol

6. Statement of Paul Wolfowitz to the House National Security Committee, Hearings on Iraq, September 16, 1998

7. Scott Ritter, "Saddam's Trap" *The New Republic,* December 21, 1998

8. "Disarming Iraq: Lessons from the UNSCOM Experience" *Policywatch* No. 377, Washington Institute for Near East Policy, March 31, 1999

9. Frank Gaffney, "Sauce for the Goose: Madeleine Albright's Lies About Iraq Make Her Another Candidate for Resignation, Impeachment: Scott Ritter for SecState?" *Washington Times,* August 27, 2003

10. Nicole Winfield, "Troops Risk Attack in Iraq's 'Red Zone'" Associated Press, April 3, 2002

11. Tim Reid and David Charter, "Pentagon Tells Bush No Evidence on WMDs" *Daily Times,* June 9, 2003

12. Julian Borger, "General Admits Chemical Weapons Intelligence Was Wrong" *The Guardian,* May 31, 2003

13. David Kay, prepared remarks, September 10, 2002

14. George W. Bush, Presidential Address to the Nation, October 8, 2002

15. Judith Miller and William J. Broad, "Some Analysts of Iraq Trailers Reject Germ Use" *New York Times,* June 7, 2003

16. Powell, *My American Journey*, p. 510–511

17. Powell, *My American Journey*, p. 511

18. Powell, *My American Journey*, p. 149

19. Benito Mussolini with Giovanni Gentile, "The Definition of Fascism" *The Italian Encyclopedia* 1932

20. William J. Bennet, "Why We Must Fight—and Now!" March 19, 2003

21. Soren Swigart, *The World at War: The Reichstag Fire* (video series) 2001

22. James Simon, *What Kind of Nation* (Simon & Schuster, 2002) p. 60

23. Simon, *What Kind of Nation*, p. 60

24. Joseph J. Ellis, *Founding Brothers* (Knopf, 2000) p. 142